MASTERING THE ART OF WHOLESALING

Paul Karasik

MASTERING THE ART OF WHOLESALING

Paul Karasik

THE WHOLESALER INSTITUTE

Also by Paul Karasik:
22 KEYS TO SALES SUCCESS
HOW TO MARKET TO HIGH-NET-WORTH HOUSESHOLDS
SEMINAR SELLING
SWEET PERSUASION
SWEET PERSUASION FOR MANAGERS
HOW TO MAKE IT BIG IN THE SEMINAR BUSINESS
BRILLIANT THOUGHTS AND PROVOCATIVE QUESTIONS

The Wholesaler Institute

Copyright © 2006 by Paul Karasik

ISBN: 2005930946

Published by:
The Wholesaler Institute, P.O. Box 4850, Weehawken, NJ 07086
To order Mastering the Art of Wholesaling by mail, include $40.00 plus $4.00 for shipping and handling, or call toll free 866-473-7600

Website: http://www.wholesalerinstitute.com

Cover Design: Frank Lacey
Interior Design: Michele DeFilippo
Editing: Lisa Smith and Evan Cooper

Contents

The Wholesaler as a Motivator

The Wholesaler as a Communicator and Presenter

Epilogue

     About Paul Karasik

     About the Wholesaler Institute

Dedication

This book is dedicated to the motivated members of financial product distribution teams, regardless of title, who are committed to raising the level of professionalism of the industry. Thank you for providing me with the opportunity to contribute to your wholesaling success.

It is also dedicated to the members of my family who have achieved success in selling based upon the philosophy of delivering value and building mutually profitable relationships. These family members include, first and foremost, my father and mother, Nat and Leah, as well as my sister Nancy, brother Rick Spelling, brother Fred, Uncle Rob, Uncle Sid, Uncle Sol, Aunt Ann, Cousin Steve, Cousin Mona, and Cousin Shelly.

And, of course, the women in my life: Samantha, Sky and Star. Without your patience, understanding and support, this book would have been impossible to write.

Acknowledgements

My sincere gratitude to all the "believers" in my life whose presence has inspired the creation of this book, as well as influenced the content including: Rose Cammerari, Jason Darling, Alex Hayes, Ron Howard, Barry Knight, Joseph Pietroski and Cindy Rowland. Thank you for your friendship, continued advice and support of my life's work and this book.

Special thanks to all of the CEOs, presidents, national sales managers, regional directors, managing directors, divisional mangers, wholesalers, inside wholesalers, key account managers and marketing professionals who offered their insights and time to The Wholesaler Institute in the research and writing of this book. The formal and informal oral and written interviews and assessments you supplied played a significant role in this book's creation. Contributors include: Nate Algiere, Kim Anderson, DeAnna Basler, Don Benson, Scott Bresky, Robert Brinkman, Mary Ann Bruce, Bob Cherichella, Gary Cohen,

David Corbin, Paul Croxton, Terry Cunningham, Larry Delaney, Mark Dunbar, John Egbert, Peter Eisenbrandt, Joe Epstein, Jim Escobedo, Mary Fau, Michael Forstl, Clay Gallagher, Dan Geilow, Jenny Godsey, Brad Hanson, Jack Hayes, Tom Hill, Leslie Honeycutt, Kris Jaenicke, Lou Jicha, Bryce Johnson, George Keith, Todd Kimmelman, Darren Kosak, Dan Kreuter, Michael Lane, Michael Lindblad, Steve Maginn, Dominic Martellaro, Mike McCoy, John Mclean, Sean McLoughlin, Sara McNeal, Chris Mierlo, Myles Morin, Kevin Myeroff, Jim Naughton, Jim Neiland, Tad Niederriter, Ellen Peters, Cheryl Potter, Liz Predergast, Dan Reinhold, Kevin Rowell, Rick Singmaster, Tim Stoddart, Bayard Tracy, Mike Vessels, Susan Viator, Scott Waters and Bob Whiting.

Thanks also to organizations that have enlisted the services of The Wholesaler Institute to grow their wholesaling teams, deliver value, and embrace the core Value-First™ concepts, strategies and techniques in this book.

These organizations include, but are not limited to: AIM Funds, Alger Funds, AllianceBernstein,

Allstate Insurance, American Skandia, Ameritas Variable Life, Asset Mark, Clark Capital Management, CM Investments, Delaware Investments, Elliot and Page, Evergreen Funds, Farmers Insurance, Federated Investors, First Asset Management, Highland Capital, Integrity Life Insurance, Keyport Life Insurance, Loring Ward, MBNA, Nations Funds, Nationwide Insurance, Pacific Life, PIMCO Funds, Pioneer Funds, RTE Asset Management, State Farm, SunAmerica, Touchstone Funds and WM Funds.

And continued thanks to my running partner, friend, colleague, mentor and consummate relationship builder James Michael Benson III.

Preface

One day in October 1987 my phone rang. An associate told me that a stock market drop of monumental proportions was taking place and that a brokerage firm was requesting my services. Their brokers needed first aid.

I was working as a general sales and marketing consultant, serving a broad array of clients, and the brokerage firm wanted me to provide intensive emotional care to the shell-shocked brokers, many of whom were metaphorically hiding under their desks. Phone calls were coming in from their irate clients who had seen their life savings evaporate, and the brokers, who didn't know what to do or say, weren't doing or saying much of anything. It was under these trying circumstances that I earned my stripes in the financial industry.

Working as a trainer and coach, I was able to help the producers rebuild their books of business and get most of them back on track. And although I'm proud of the rebuilding I was able to achieve, something of a much higher order happened. The three-month engagement changed my life and redirected my professional future.

The producers and managers I met enthralled me. The brokers came from all walks of life. While they worked in the capital of finance, many came from modest families in Brooklyn and the Bronx. Through hard work, entrepreneurial spirit, and the application of excellent sales and marketing skills, they were able to achieve what their friends from the old neighborhood could only dream about.

I fell in love with the excitement of the financial industry and the people in it. There was an importance and gravity to their work that captured my heart, soul and imagination. My admiration and respect for the professionals I trained and coached made me decide to concentrate my practice in the financial industry.

The sales strategies I taught, which focused on relationships, were a perfect fit for my clients, regardless of product or distribution channel. My professional mission statement evolved effortlessly and seemed to write itself: To help financial professionals sell and market their products and services more successfully.

Almost immediately, I began working with the wholesaling side of the business. My father and many other members of my immediate family were salespeople. Wholesalers exhibited many of the traits, skills and personality characteristics of old-school salespeople, and I found it easy to relate to their lifestyle and personalities. As my work with wholesalers progressed, I created The Wholesaler Institute to provide state-of-the-art training, coaching and resources that enable wholesaling teams to produce more sales. We have been successful in addressing the needs and opportunities that have been presented by the changing financial marketplace.

Commoditization of products, a volatile market, and more intense levels of regulation and compliance have produced a variety of issues making many long-standing wholesaling strategies and techniques less effective. Among the wholesalers' clients, the situation is even worse. Much of the sales training and professional development that once existed in the retail distribution channels has been eliminated.

The convergence of these factors has created an incredible opportunity for wholesalers who are ready to seize the opportunity and deliver real value to each of their relationships. I believe many of the successful wholesaling teams of the future will be positioned as coaches, consultants and trainers.

For anyone who has been in the financial industry since 1987, it's an understatement to say there have been lots of changes. But there is one fundamental truth that will never change. Successful selling depends on creating, expanding and maintaining relationships.

This truth has been at the core of all of my work as a consultant in the financial industry. It is the essential message of this book, too. Relationships are the alpha and omega of achieving sales success. It was true in October of 1987 and it is true today.

As my dad said to me when I was developing my skills in sales, "Son, always sell yourself first, and your products and services will sell themselves."

Keep your eye and your attention on your relationships, and the sales will take care of themselves. I wish you success today, tomorrow, and for the length of your career.

Introduction

This book is for you: the financial professional who is an intermediary between the financial product manufacturer and the person who sells that product to the end user. Your daily challenge is how to influence the decision-making of others to make your product one of those chosen for sale.

The book is also for other members of the wholesaling team. These key team members include inside wholesalers, key account managers and various product marketing specialists. Your unique relationship skills and expertise play a critical and often deciding role in achieving and surpassing sales goals.

And it's also for the leaders who form the connective tissue between the field and the home office. You may be the national sales manager, vice president of sales, divisional manager, channel manager, inside sales manager, training manager or marketing manager. Your vision for the future and your commitment to professional development may lead you to place this book in the hands of other readers.

My purpose in the pages that follow is to make a contribution to the financial industry by raising the level of wholesaling professionalism, one wholesaler at a time. The book should provide as much value to the seasoned pro as it does to the recently promoted inside wholesaler.

If you are experienced and successful, the book will give you refinement and renewal, and it will remind you of what makes you as effective as you are. If you are new to the field, it will provide not only skill development but a guidance system for lifelong professional growth.

The concepts, strategies and techniques presented will ground you in the immutable laws of relationship building. Properly implemented, they will enable you to reap the financial rewards as well as the personal satisfaction your profession offers.

To make scenarios come to life, I've included a variety of examples. Product references may include insurance, mutual funds, separately managed accounts, annuities and alternative investments. Your clients are referred to as producers, financial advisors, reps, clients and investment advisors. I will refer to what you do as selling, even though it involves much more.

Mastering the Art of Wholesaling is designed not as a training manual but as a guide. I do not elaborate on every aspect of wholesaling. Instead, the chapters touch on, summarize and crystallize the best practices of the most successful wholesalers in the business. The short format is designed for the busy wholesalers I've come to know and thoroughly enjoy working with.

This book is a reflection of my nearly twenty years of personal experience in training and coaching a wide variety of wholesalers and managers. It also reflects a series of comprehensive interviews my organization conducted with members of wholesaling teams to glean a more complete view of the industry.

Many of the teams we've worked with have succeeded in raising wholesaling to a high-minded profession. These teams exhibit the traits, qualities and skills I discuss in this book. I hope you will see yourself, your ideas and your aspirations shining through these pages.

The title of this book underscores my fundamental belief about wholesaling. It is as much an art as a science. If wholesaling were purely a science, success would be a function of information, knowledge and logic. In such a world, the actuaries, money managers, product development teams and compliance managers would be out in the field.

But wholesaling is not a science. Even when logic and reason are working against you, such as when your product performs poorly or is out of favor — you are expected to bring in the numbers. And you do! At those times, like Houdini, a great wholesaler will find a way to open a seemingly locked door to a significant producer. They'll even have mastered the art of being welcomed by an advisor on a routine sales call. There's no science in having a winning personal presence.

Because you are reading this book, I assume you have made a decision. You have decided to pursue excellence that is beyond the ordinary in order to achieve the extraordinary. Congratulations on your decision to learn and to maximize your potential. Thank you for allowing me to contribute to your success in your quest for *Mastering the Art of Wholesaling.*

The Wholesaler as a Sales Professional

~1~
Your Ideal Prospect

*D*o you know your ideal prospect? Can you describe him or her in precise terms? Any prospect may turn into a client through a single transaction, but ideal prospects are those who deliver serious volume, serve as ongoing resources for new business and become welcome, enjoyable working partners. Use these four criteria to define your ideal prospect in specific detail:

1. What are his or her personal traits, qualities and characteristics? Like most people, wholesalers interact more effectively with some prospects than with others. That's human nature. It's not as if you

can't or won't sell to all types of people, but it's much easier to establish rapport and relationships with some types than with others. So consider age, background and personality type. You may find it easier to sell to people of your own age; others prefer selling to an older or younger group.

Values are key. If you have a strong commitment to health and fitness, for example, you will find it easier to relate to people who share these values. If spirituality or religion is a high priority in your life, you will probably relate well to like-minded prospects. Similarly, if you are outgoing and gregarious, you probably related better to someone like you rather than to someone who is shy or more introspective.

Connecting to people who are like you in key ways simply requires less effort than working with "strangers." Since you spend more time with prospects and clients than with family and friends, doesn't it make sense to initiate and maintain relationships with people you find easy to deal with? You don't always have a choice, of course, but when you do, consider the importance of personal rapport and ease of relationship.

2. What is your ideal prospect's business model? Does it match your product? If you are selling a fee-based product, for instance, has the prospect converted to a fee-based business or is his or her business still commission-based? Also, is the prospect capable of doing significant business with you? This is particularly important if you are selling products designed for the high-net-worth market.

3. Do your ideal prospects want to expand their business? Some prospects are merely treading water, seeking to maintain the status quo. Even worse, they may be allowing their business to shrink. Growth-oriented prospects are ideal. Their growth mode gives you an opportunity to supply needed products and to serve as a resource, helping them to increase business. In short, an ideal prospect has a business plan that has room for you.

4. Are your prospects willing and able to refer you to others like themselves? Referral generation, an integral strategy for growing a retail business,

should be part of your business development plan, too. Remember: Third-party endorsements make powerful selling points.

Before approaching your next prospect, ask yourself: Would I enjoy having a long-term relationship with this person? Is this person capable of doing significant ongoing business? Does this person intend to grow the business? Will this person refer other, similar producers to me?

If your answer to these questions is yes, you have found an ideal prospect.

EXECUTIVE SUMMARY

Before you can maximize your sales you must excel in identifying your ideal prospect. Remember it takes as much effort sell a button as it does to sell the whole suit.

~2~
What You're
Really *Selling*
Are Solutions

Here's a depressing fact of financial wholesaling life: Nobody wants the mutual funds, annuities, life insurance policies, separately managed accounts, hedge funds, or any of the other financial products you sell. Yet, every day, millions of dollars of these products are sold by your customers to their clients. Here's why: While no one wants the products, everyone wants what products deliver. That's why successful wholesalers think, sell, and deliver benefits and solutions.

What are the benefits of the products you sell? There really are only three: wealth accumulation, wealth preservation, and wealth transfer. Some products, like mutual funds, fall cleanly into one category. Others, like many insurance products, fall into a few. Your first step, then, is to think about the major benefit your product delivers, or the solution it provides. Then focus your sales effort on that generic product benefit, not your specific product. The product-specific message should come at the end — almost as an afterthought. If your product is competitive, you'll earn your share of business.

Naturally, it's easier and more efficient to speak with producers who already are convinced of the benefits that come from selling the types of products you wholesale. When you meet with them, sell the benefits of increasing their involvement with your product class. Ultimately, they and you will sell more of your particular product.

When it comes time to sell your specific product, don't fall into the trap of concentrating on product features. A focus on benefits or solutions pays off even when discussing a specific product. Remember, features are what your product has; benefits are what it does and solutions are the problems the product solves. Selling features instead of benefits is like talking about the milling techniques used to make flour instead of concentrating on the incredibly delicious cakes the flour can be used to make.

Unfortunately, features are what your home office product specialists talk about all the time. Features are the obsession of marketing departments, the focus of too many sales meetings and, ironically, the ultimate distraction for sales success.

Here are some examples of feature-talk — and what reps and clients are actually thinking when you are talking.

You say: "Our funds are passively managed." And they think: "Great. I'm not even sure what that means, but it sounds weak. And why should I even care?"

You say: "Our annuity has a short four-year surrender period." And they think: "Fine, if you say so. But what good does that do me?"

You say: "We offer institutional-quality asset allocation." And they think: "That's nice, but I'm not sure I want to be institutionalized."

You — or, more accurately, your marketing pieces — say: "This fund seeks consistent daily returns, before fees and expenses, that are 120 percent of the inverse of the price movement of the most recently issued thirty-year U.S. Treasury Bond." And they think: "Huh???"

It's not that the information contained in features isn't valuable and shouldn't be mentioned. The important point is that wholesalers should not take their sales focus from the marketing department, which typically knows very little about sales and often resents salespeople. Your job is to put benefits ahead of features.

To do that, associate every product feature with a benefit and write a script showing those associations. Many of these benefits appear obvious, like excellent long-term returns or impressive ratings from a company like Standard and Poor's or A.M. Best. These benefits appear obvious to you and the financial professionals you serve, but they may not be obvious to the consumer.

Second, after you have identified the benefits, write down how you will help your advisor clients communicate these benefits to their clients and prospects. Give them short benefit-oriented presentations they can use with qualified prospects.

Remember that many financial professionals enjoy the technical aspects of the financial business more than selling. That's where they need your help. The more guidance you give them in how to sell your product by focusing on benefits, the more they are likely to sell. Help them identify ideal prospects for the benefits your products can provide, and give them simple benefit scripts. Your clients will sell more when they can replace feature-talk with benefit-talk, and focus on issues like stability, security and retirement dreams.

But benefit-talk does not come naturally to most financial professionals, so help them out. Make it a habit never to utter a feature without connecting it to a benefit. That's what selling benefits means. Every sales call and every presentation must drip with benefits from beginning to end. Nobody wants what you sell. They want the benefits. That's what you need to sell.

EXECUTIVE SUMMARY

Give your presentations the "So What?" test. When you are presenting technical features of your product, connect the features with the appropriate benefits by asking, "So what?" and giving the answer in terms of benefits.

~3~
The Perfect Question

Successful wholesalers are always looking for the magic combinations of words that will turn a prospect into a buyer. I know that combination and it's only five words long. Let me share it with you:

"How may I help you?"

Disappointed? Is the question too simplistic? Too short? Let me tell you why it works.

It accomplishes several things. First, it drives home the weakness of a product-focused sales approach because no client ever will answer the question by saying "I could really use another variable annuity," or "I was wondering where I could find another small-cap fund." You and I both know that product availability at any given moment is the least important area in which a client can use help.

Second, the question demonstrates your empathy for the client. By showing that you care, you demonstrate friendship and loyalty, and for a brief moment you banish the loneliness that comes with being a financial advisor.

Asking the question achieves a third positive result by uncovering your client's precise needs and concerns. If you ask the question sincerely and listen intently to the answer, your client will open up and get past posturing and game-playing.

The answers you receive when you ask, "How may I help you?" will range from the simple to the complex:

"I need to organize my business better."

"I need more high-net-worth clients."

"I wish I had more time with my family."

"I need to create a more effective team."

"I need help running my seminars."

It really doesn't matter how the question is answered because the answer is going to reveal the exact way in which you can contribute to the producer's life. When you provide the help your client needs, you add value that will propel you to the position of preferred wholesaler. And that's always the best place to be.

With dedication and creativity, you can provide limitless solutions for the problems your clients name. You may be able to solve the problems yourself, or you may wish to enlist the support of your organization. Sometimes referring your client to an outside consultant or to a training program, seminar or book can be just what's needed.

Independent producers, of course, rely on the help of outsiders like you. But even employee financial advisors welcome your assistance because they typically have far less support today than they did just a few years ago. With far more opportunities to offer advice, support and resources, isn't it time you asked, "How may I help you?"

EXECUTIVE SUMMARY

Altruistic egotism is the ultimate wholesaling philosophy. Take care of the needs of the producer and he or she will take care of you.

~4~
The Only Sales Script That Works

Great wholesalers are prepared. They understand that preparation is the difference between success and SUCCESS. And of all the steps wholesalers take to ready themselves for their daily encounters, the most important involve preparing the right words.

Knowing what to say beforehand is called scripting, and top-producing wholesalers are armed in advance with the words that are most likely to achieve the desired results. While a perfect script will not guarantee a perfect response, it will improve your chances enormously.

If scripts are so great, why don't more wholesalers use them? Why do so many resist embracing a tool that will help them succeed? The answer is simple: bad programming. When most people hear "sales script" they think of annoying and incompetent telemarketers who call us at dinnertime and read a canned spiel like a robot. Through the magic of technology, these dodos have been replaced by recorded sales pitches. No wonder you have a negative view of scripts!

The best scripts, of course, are invisible. Broadway shows, movies and your favorite TV programs are all scripted (yes, even lots of the reality shows), but you'd never know it by the professional performances. You, the audience, remember being moved by the spoken words of Tom Hanks, Al Pacino or Julia Roberts. You don't think of them as reciting written words. Great performers are capable of delivering well-written lines over and over again, producing the same audience response time after time.

The same is true of wholesaling. Great scripts employed by great wholesalers are invisible. In other words, if you use a script properly, your audience will be unaware that you're using a script and they will be moved to action by your words. It is the responsibility of the great wholesaler to identify the great words and deliver them masterfully. Some of your scripts might remain fairly constant, such as the one that describes the benefit of offering your particular core product to clients. Other scripts might require updating, such as the one that tells how your product compares to a recently released competitive product.

Dynamite scripts come from a variety of sources. The first is you. Remember when an advisor asked why he should sell your product over a better-ranked competitor's, and in that moment you spouted a brilliant analogy or metaphor? The advisor's eyes lit up, and you nailed a nice piece of business. Remember other times when just the right word or phrase tumbled out at just the right time? Capture those powerful words and write them down. Unless you record them, they will be forgotten and lost forever. After writing them down, you will then be able to memorize them, deliver them again at the appropriate moment, and produce equally impressive results.

When you are seeking the perfect words for a presentation or situation, remember the wisdom of Ralph Waldo Emerson:

> A man should learn to detect and watch that gleam of light which flashes across his own mind from within, more than the luster of the firmament of bards and sages. Yet he dismisses without notice his thought, because it is his. In every work of genius we recognize our own rejected thoughts; they come back to us with a certain alienated majesty.

The second source of dynamite scripts is your colleagues, especially those who put up the numbers. I've never met a top-producing wholesaler who did not identify and employ brilliant scripts. Even though there is always healthy competition among wholesalers, ask them what they say in a given situation and I bet they will share their script with you.

A third source: Sometimes you'll hear a colleague at another firm say something brilliant during a presentation. Let your ego take a back seat to your bank account. Adopt, adapt, and apply.

Top producers understand that brilliant words, brilliantly delivered, produce brilliant results. Yes, the words themselves have no power without you. But at the same time, remember that you, without the words, have no power either. Find the most powerful words and use them.

EXECUTIVE SUMMARY

The student plays the instrument, the musician plays the music, the master plays the audience.

~5~
Doubling Your Production Is Easy with Modeling

There's an easy and accessible route to dramatically improving your performance and sales numbers. Dressed up in B-school phraseology, the concept is known as modeling: emulating someone whose behavior you admire, largely because it works. Successful modeling involves four steps:

1. Identifying the most successful wholesaler you know. This should be someone you're somewhat familiar with, but not necessarily the most popular wholesaler you know or the one you like best. Choose someone who sells products similar to yours in a market similar to yours.

2. Visualizing this model wholesaler. Create a mental image of this person and picture how he or she operates professionally.

3. Identifying the traits, qualities, characteristics, and skills that contribute to the effectiveness of this wholesaler. List them, and be as specific as possible. For example, don't just list "well-organized." Go deeper and identify the strategies or techniques used, such as "plans all appointments 90 days in advance," or "reviews all notes before every appointment." Don't just say "persistent." Identify how this trait is implemented. For example, perhaps the wholesaler combines face-to-face appointments with telephone and e-mail. If you say "great communicator," be sure to identify the communication skills used, such as "uses questions effectively" or "listens well."

4. Developing the personal traits you are comfortable emulating, and implementing the specific strategies and techniques your model wholesaler uses. The easiest way to succeed with this process is to go to your model and ask for advice and help. If you

ask with respect and demonstrate a sincere desire to learn, most people will respond favorably.

If you approach another wholesaler for coaching in a specific area, be sure to offer something in return. This may be a book or an audio program you found helpful. At the very least, offer to take your success model out to lunch or dinner at a convenient time.

Modeling is a dynamic path to performance improvement. If you can identify the traits and habits of the most successful wholesalers in the business and then develop and practice those traits yourself, you are bound to achieve greatness.

EXECUTIVE SUMMARY
Emulate the traits, qualities, skills, and habits of great wholesalers and you will quickly become one.

~6~

Invest in
Your Top 20

Time is your No. 1 resource. Your production, in fact, is determined solely by two factors of time management: who you spend your time with and how you spend that time.

To help maximize the time available to you, list the top 20 percent of your client list based on their revenue to you. Have you just taken over a territory? Make sure your home office gives you those figures.

Use the Top 20 as a basis for managing your time and territory. This elite group probably contributes most of your total sales — as much as 80 percent, if the usual rule-of-thumb guideline applies — so concentrate your efforts here. The guiding principle when dealing with these most-important clients is to concentrate on what and how you can contribute to those who contribute most to you.

Therefore, don't call on your Top 20 just to schmooze or to hound them for more business. Your best deserve more than that. Instead, become a welcome guest in their lives. Center your conversations on their needs, concerns, challenges and objectives. Learn how you can help them build their business and improve their lives in other ways. Become obsessed with contributing to your Top 20, and your Top 20 will contribute more to you.

EXECUTIVE SUMMARY
*The people most qualified to
do business with you in the future
are those who have done business
with you in the past.*

~7~
The Ultimate Selling Skill

*T*oo often, wholesalers ignore the ultimate sell-ing skill. It's a skill that gives users a competi-tive advantage, lets you bring value into every rela-tionship and makes every encounter enjoyable. When you master this skill, which represents 80 percent of the selling process, you attract relationships effort-lessly. What is this ultimate selling skill? It's listening.

Wholesalers, of course, want to speak. You're pumped up about your product, and rarin' to talk about it. Unfortunately, most reps aren't waiting to hear another product pitch by a zealous wholesaler. If you don't believe me, notice how many attendees are reading newspapers during the obligatory wholesaler presentations at the next wholesaler-sponsored conference you attend.

Reps would much rather have a wholesaler who listens to them than one talks to them. When you listen, you communicate a simple message to clients and prospects: That they are important and that you care.

Successful wholesaling needs relationships. Relationships are based on feelings. We initiate relationships with people who make us feel good. We want relationships that satisfy a need or desire. Your ability to create and maintain relationships will grow in proportion to your ability to make people feel good every time they come in contact with you. When you listen, you make people feel good.

Listening is difficult for a variety of reasons. First, you would rather talk about what's important to you. You want to sell stuff! Second, it's no fun. You are not the center of attention when you listen. Third, it takes a lot of patience. Most people can listen to and understand speech three or four times faster than the average person speaks; this creates lag time, leading to impatience. And you've probably heard what's being said several hundred times before. Fourth, listening can be difficult for technical reasons, such as an accent or a speech impediment or a noisy room.

So what's your incentive to become a great listener? How about money? The better your listening skills, the more money you are going to make. Imagine two wholesalers, with equally performing products, knocking on the door of the guy in the corner office. One wholesaler is an excellent listener, skilled at getting others to share; the other wholesaler is a talker. Which one is more likely to be invited in? Which one are you?

EXECUTIVE SUMMARY

Listening isn't passive. You must actively pay attention to what is being said, probe for the rep's deeper meaning, and verbally confirm that you understand his or her underlying needs and concerns.

~8~
The
Joint Call

The secret to persuading reps to follow your suggestions is to be a leader. And leadership involves doing, not just talking. Providing reps with insights into positioning your product and winning the sale goes only so far. You've got to show them how to do it. And the best way to show, not merely tell, is to go on joint sales calls. When you lead by example, you demonstrate that you're for real, that you're committed to the rep's success and that your behavior is worth emulating — because it works!

Go out on a few sales calls with your top-producing reps, and they will quickly know what to say and how to say it. They may not be as good as you at first, but they will be a lot better than if you just handed them a script.

Start scheduling those joint sales calls.

EXECUTIVE SUMMARY
*Great generals don't send their troops
into battle, they lead them.*

~9~
Harnessing Your
Inner Monster

There's an old movie whose characters every great wholesaler should emulate. It's the black-and-white horror film *Night of the Living Dead,* which is worth seeing despite its embarrassingly low production values, predictable plot and "B" actors. The monsters in the movie are kind of pathetic. They are zombies dressed like hobos, and their primary on-camera activity is walking slowly in a lock-step rhythm toward their victims. They are hardly frightening and even border on the comical.

Their one enviable quality is their dogged determination. Their eyes are wide-open, and they rarely look to the right or left. Throughout the film, the zombies are assaulted by bullets, bats and other assorted missiles and projectiles. Regardless of their wounds, they remain unfazed and focused. They continue plodding onward. They are impervious to the assaults.

Normally, I wouldn't like to be compared to a zombie. But their ability to keep marching forward, steadily and fearlessly, is admirable. In fact, if I were putting together a world-class wholesaling team and could choose between a candidate with a Mensa IQ but no inner monster-like drive and a candidate who wasn't the brightest bulb in the chandelier but possessed the heart and soul of a monster, I would most certainly choose the latter.

Monster wholesalers maintain a laser-beam focus on their objectives. Lesser wholesalers often complain to their colleagues about lack of marketing support, poor product performance, or noncompetitive features. Monster wholesalers don't waste time or energy on matters they cannot change. They don't turn right or left and dissipate energy that detracts from their objectives.

Fortunately, everyone has a monster inside. It can be a source of strength and a foundation for achievement when the going gets tough. Unleash the monster and keep moving forward.

EXECUTIVE SUMMARY
Monster wholesalers maintain a
laser-beam focus on their objectives.

~10~
The Funnel

*O*ccupations seem to run in families. Some families produce fire fighters, others doctors, and a few, scholars. My family produced salespeople.

My father, his two brothers and his sister's husband, my mother, my sister and my two brothers-in-law have all spent most of their working lives in sales. My dad died at age 83 on his way to a meet with a prospect. He loved selling and was pure "old school" in the way he endeared himself to the people he sold to.

One day when I was in my early teens and actively searching for my life path, I discussed with my dad the concept of making a living. I was passionate about a variety of areas, including science and music, but I felt insecure about those two as a vocational direction. It was during the discussion that my dad, in just a few words, handed me a concept that gave me a feeling of security and provided a seed that took hold and generated a truly rewarding career. After I voiced my confusion and inability to choose what I wanted to major in, he looked at me and said, "Son, learn how to sell, and you will never have to worry about making a living."

Teenagers have a habit of discounting what their parents tell them. But looking into his eyes at that moment, I knew my father had given me an incredible security blanket. I didn't know much about selling or if I would enjoy it. But I liked the concept of never having to worry.

My father pointed out a few other valuable features of professional selling. He said, "The wonderful thing about selling is that you have unlimited potential. You control your destiny. You can make as much money as you choose."

Then he talked about the core and immutable concept of successful selling. "It's all a numbers game. It's really that simple. The more people you talk to, the more you will sell."

My heart and soul resonated to this philosophy of rugged individualism, and his advice would reside unfaded in my memory.

After I spent years in the music business and assorted trivial occupational pursuits in my twenties, his words guided me back to my calling, first as a successful salesperson and then as a sales consultant, trainer and coach.

My dad gave me much sage selling wisdom through his words and his actions, but the most important remains the concept I call the funnel. What is true for any sales pursuit will be true for your wholesaling: your results will be determined by how well you fill your funnel.

The funnel defines selling at a very basic level. Here's how it works. First you approach lots of people. That's the wide mouth at the top of the funnel. Next, you interview them and determine if they are qualified to do business with you. That is the middle section of the funnel, which is considerably narrower.

Much of your wholesaling activity is generated with the producers in the narrow end of the funnel and the stem. These are the qualified people who present a viable opportunity to do business with you in the near future.

New business is what finally drips out from the bottom. To produce sales, you must continually fill the funnel. Sales slumps are usually the result of failing to keep the funnel filled. You can't get stuff out of the bottom if you don't put stuff in the top. Old timers like my dad had it right. It is a numbers game.

The funnel concept defines wholesaling and your destiny.

EXECUTIVE SUMMARY
"It's all a numbers game. It's really that simple. The more people you talk to, the more you will sell."

~11~
The Most Powerful
Closing Strategy

While sales books and training programs abound with closing techniques, few actually work in the world of wholesaling. Here's one that does: the third-party endorsement.

That shouldn't come as a surprise, since there's nothing more powerful than having a friend or expert talk positively about a product or service. After all, wouldn't you believe the enthusiasm of one of your golf buddies about a new set of clubs over the explanation of the golf-shop salesman? Someone whose opinion you value can sell you on any product or service better than any advertisement.

To sell more and open more doors, therefore, you must cultivate third-party endorsements. Here's how to do it:

First, go beyond having a good reputation. Create a fantastic reputation. That takes time, so start immediately. You don't have a minute to lose. Do the right thing at all times. Go beyond your clients' expectations — every time. Since you can't control product performance, control everything about your own performance. Do everything you have to do in order to earn the right to be endorsed.

Second, ask your angels for help. Doing a great job isn't enough; your clients have to tell people that you've done a great job. But since your clients aren't mind readers and don't know what you need or expect from them, help them out. Tell them you'd like endorsements. If you don't ask (and you can do this in a nice, non-pushy way), you don't get. It's up to you. Create a list of clients from whom you would feel comfortable asking for help.

Third, arrange a way for your angels to provide you with endorsements. If someone the angel knows has a specific problem where your advice would be helpful, one effective technique is to arrange a conference call that includes your prospect, your angel and you. Another excellent technique is a face-to-face meeting of the three of you over lunch or dinner. Both ways allow for a real-time endorsement of your services and the value of including your products in the mix.

Your objective at the end of the phone call or gathering is to set up a one-to-one meeting with the prospect.

The easiest way to open closed doors is to have someone inside open them. Review your client list, identify your angels, and set up telephone and face-to-face meetings. The third party endorsement is the most powerful means of opening new business relationships from the inside. Include this strategy in your marketing plan and you are guaranteed to reap the rewards.

EXECUTIVE SUMMARY
Suppose you overheard the following statements, which one would you believe: "I'm a great guy" or "Joe's a great guy." 'Nuff said. There's nothing more powerful in sales than the third-party endorsement.

~12~
Wholesaler or Order Taker?

Some wholesalers are lucky. They sell a product that is clearly superior in its field, whether due to performance, current investment fashion or because it's the first one with some cool bells and whistles. Whatever the reason, when the product is right, it takes little or no effort on the wholesaler's part to put great numbers up on the board.

While a product's blazing popularity may be a great blessing in terms of creating revenue short term, it has the unfortunate potential of creating a huge negative in the long term by giving the wholesaler a false sense of his/her abilities. When sales simply fall into your lap, you are not wholesaling; you're just taking orders. Order taking is an administrative process, not a selling skill.

But what happens if your luck changes and your hot product suddenly cools? Will your wholesaling skills still be there to take over when order-taking is no longer enough? Remember, when a muscle isn't exercised, it atrophies. When you become complacent and rely on outside forces to propel your sales, you expose yourself to the possibility of severely reducing your value in the marketplace. It's great to be in the right place at the right time. But great times are the best time to work on your selling skills. When times are great, set your goals higher.

Expand your rep base. Cross-sell products that are not in high demand. You'll stay sharp and keep your edge. And when the market and your product's competitive advantage turn against you, as they always do, you'll be the one to survive and thrive. You will never lose confidence in your abilities, and your potential to earn will continue to expand.

Take pride in your creativity and your ability to create and maintain profitable relationships. Conduct regular self-evaluations. Ask yourself, "Did I earn this sale or was I an order taker?" If you continually strive to be a great wholesaler, you will never have to worry about job security.

EXECUTIVE SUMMARY
Great times are the best times to cross-sell and expand your base.

~13~
Two Wholesalers
Walk into a Bar

*A*s a consultant for a large mutual fund organization, I was traveling with wholesalers and delivering one of my core training programs for advisors called "How to Market to High-Net-Worth Clients." My objective was not only to help advisors but to be an ambassador for the fund company and drive more business to the wholesalers.

I delivered the program at large branch offices of a wirehouse. The advisors who attended spanned the entire spectrum of production levels. The goal of my program was to attract elite advisors who are difficult to reach, so that wholesalers could gain access to them. Normally, access to these advisors was extremely limited; nothing short of a fire alarm could pry these top producers out of their offices.

Working closely with the fund company and the wirehouse's marketing department, I designed a program that had the appeal needed to achieve that goal. We succeeded in filling the seats at our programs with many of the specific producers we had targeted. Most of the wholesalers were experienced and used my program to successfully initiate and build profitable relationships.

It was at one of these presentations that I worked with a wholesaler whom I will fondly refer to as a mismatch, although I have heard sales managers refer to this kind of wholesaler in much more colorful terms.

As the wholesaler and I set up for the presentation, the sales manager at this branch office assured us it was very unlikely that any of the heavy hitters would attend. They would be too busy on the phone and unavailable. If they did attend, it would be for just a few minutes; they definitely would not sit through the entire program.

As good fortune would have it, the most successful rep in the office wandered in just after I had begun. The wholesaler looked at her and then turned to me with a "we're in luck" wink. Not only did she stay for more than a few minutes, she actively participated in the entire presentation, asked engaging questions, and stayed after the other participants returned to their offices. And then, to our surprise and delight, she invited us both back to the corner office where she generated millions of dollars of production each year.

For the next hour we bantered about the viability and profitability of implementing the marketing strategies I had introduced. She was open to possibilities, exceedingly friendly and completely sincere in her intentions. I was elated, knowing the presentation had succeeded in opening a door that until that day had been bolted shut to practically all wholesalers.

Then something happened that dramatically illustrates why wholesalers need a specific personality trait. I would like to believe that what happened was an anomaly, one that had never happened before or since, but I know better.

As we prepared to wind down this ideal conversation, she said to the wholesaler, "I'd love more information on this high-net-worth marketing strategy." This would require the wholesaler's support and give him the perfect opportunity to expand his relationship with her.

"Wow," I thought to myself, "our value-added program is unfolding exactly as we had envisioned it."

But rather than picking up on her lead, seizing this perfect moment and setting up a time and place for the next meeting, the wholesaler gathered his briefcase and marched to the door.

Then, perhaps out of an unconscious desire to give the wholesaler another cue and an opportunity to redeem himself, she said, "I'm impossible to get hold of, I don't answer e-mail from any vendors, and I specifically never see or return calls to wholesalers." This clarion call also fell on inept ears. In an instant we were standing outside her now shut office door.

I was astounded. The wholesaler didn't quite understand the magnitude of the lost opportunity. His only remark: "That was a good meeting."

This sad, but true, episode reminds me of an old sales joke. Two salespeople meet at the end of the day. One says to the other, "How did your day go?" The second responds, "I had a lot of good conversations." To which the first salesperson replies, "Yeah, I didn't make any sales either."

EXECUTIVE SUMMARY

Wholesalers, I beg of you, carpe diem. Seize the day! Seize that precious moment to close on your next step.

The
Wholesaler
as a
Manager

~14~
You're
the CEO...

Do you think of yourself as part of a selling team? Do you think of yourself as a member of a large corporation? Do you think of yourself as a salesperson? All are true. But if you want to take control of your professional future and exceed your sales goals every quarter and every year, you must also think of yourself as a chief executive officer.

The truth is, you are not only a CEO, you are the CEO of a large business that results in sales of hundreds of millions of dollars. That's not a metaphor, it's reality.

As a CEO, you must employ strategic thinking to guide your tactical actions. Responsibilities, philosophies and activities vary greatly from one CEO to the next, but every CEO is responsible for vision. The CEO must "see" where his company is going. His vision is a picture of the future. It's not quantified production goals, but the overall strategies needed to achieve those goals.

A well-defined wholesaler vision might be: Providing ideal, highly qualified advisors with a continuous stream of strategies, techniques, resources and products for improving their businesses and their lives.

The most powerful vision statements are written. Putting the vision on paper forces you to crystallize your thoughts and cement the vision in your consciousness. It also enables you to communicate it to other members of your sales team, your clients and your manager.

Tailor your vision statement to your unique talents and approach to wholesaling. If your wholesaling team already has a vision statement, you might need to customize it to fit your personality, territory or target market.

You're the CEO. You must write, internalize and communicate your vision of future success. It will become a compass for your "company." You will manifest in the future what you focus on today.

EXECUTIVE SUMMARY

Leadership always begins with a vision of the future. How do you see yourself and your team achieving your sales goals?

~15~
...So You're Gonna Need a Map

Can you imagine driving across the country to a place you have never been without a road map? I don't think so. Chances are you would pull out your road atlas or go online and print out a precise route that will get you where you want to go in the most efficient way possible.

But many wholesalers attempt to achieve their professional goals without a written plan. Just as bad, they often devise a plan but don't follow it or neglect to revise it.

If you don't have a business plan, here are eight reasons to write one:

1. Writing a plan forces you to clarify issues, such as what you are going to sell and to whom.
2. It helps you identify necessary business steps, just as a map helps you plan stops for meals and rest on a cross-country drive.
3. Your business plan allows you to visualize success. Most world-class athletes use visualization to prepare for and succeed in their endeavors. They mentally "see" themselves crossing the finish line first, scoring the winning goal or pitching strikes. Your business plan helps you create a mental picture of what you intend to accomplish. Your plan might include a goal of three appointments a day and two seminars a week.
4. It assists you in staying on course. Losing focus and veering off the road is all too easy. Taking the time to write a good plan will give you the highest likelihood of achieving your goal. A good plan that you actually follow is far better than a perfect plan that you ignore.
5. Business plans make adjustments easier. Think of your plan as a point of reference that you can modify

as needed. If you were following your road map and a snowstorm was forecast, you could choose a different route. A business plan also can be refined or modified to accommodate unforeseen circumstances that affect your territory or products.

6. It permits you to enlist others to advise you. If you have a manager who is an effective mentor or coach, you can request a review of your plan and solicit valuable feedback. Smart people recognize the importance of asking smart people to guide them. If your manager can't give you advice, show your plan to colleagues you respect or to other wholesalers who have handled your territory or similar territories.

7. A business plan helps you to align yourself with organizational goals. Your plan will help you adjust to new products being rolled out, territory changes or shifts in management. Submit your business plan to your manager for review even if that is not required. Your manager may give you an organizational perspective that helps you direct your energies as productively as possible.

8. Your plan will uncover educational needs. For example, you may need to become more knowledgeable about a product, a new distribution channel or a brokerage firm with which you recently signed a distribution contract. If you're handling a fee-based product, you may need to learn more about how to help advisors make the transition to a fee-based model.

Your business plan won't guarantee your success, but it will increase the chance of achieving your goals. It is meant to be a living document to which you refer often on your path toward your monthly, quarterly, and yearly goals. Your business plan is your road map to success.

EXECUTIVE SUMMARY
If you want to put yourself on the map, publish your own map.

~16~
The Perfect Territory

*E*very wholesaler has a dream: To be given the perfect territory. This mythic turf abounds with top producers who welcome you warmly every time you visit their conveniently located offices, demanding lots of what you sell and little of your time. Your only challenge is determining your ever-increasing quota — which you handily meet each year.

OK, now you can awake from the dream. The perfect territory does not exist. But very good territories do exist, and invariably what makes a territory good is not geography or luck but a wholesaler who knows the secret of maximizing its potential. The secret? Spending time with significant reps, which are those reps qualified to do significant business with you.

If you don't have enough reps who fit this description, spend more time creating strategies and techniques that will open the doors to finding them. It takes as much effort to initiate and maintain relationships with insignificant clients as it does to work with those who will give you significant business. Concentrate on significant producers and territory perfection will follow.

EXECUTIVE SUMMARY

Whether your territory is Manhattan, Missouri or Manitoba, it's only as perfect as the producers with whom you spend your time.

~17~
Time
Is Power

*T*he life of a wholesaler is filled with activities and responsibilities. To maximize your success, you must employ a system to manage them. The underlying principle of effective time management is simple: Identify your goals and spend your time engaged in the activities that will enable you to achieve them.

The beauty of wholesaling is that the metrics are simple. You're rated highly if you sell a lot of stuff; you're rated poorly if you sell a little. That simplicity is beautiful. Like the score of a football game, how good you are is not up for debate and opinions don't matter. The numbers tell the story. And the best way to hit your numbers — and go beyond them — is to spend and manage your time well. Time management, in fact, will determine your success. Great wholesalers know this and are prudent to the point of being miserly with their time. How you spend your precious minutes each day will determine your numbers.

How should you spend your time? Spend it with producers who currently write significant business with you and are capable of writing more, and with producers who are qualified to do business with you. When you're with them, help them improve their lives.

View every activity that is not part of this vision as a diversion, obstacle or deterrent keeping you from achieving your sales goals. Eliminate or delegate everything that is not part of the vision. Some of these peripheral activities — scheduling appointments, mailing marketing pieces, returning phone calls — are necessary, but can be assigned to your internal wholesaler or an assistant at headquarters. In some cases, you might want to hire an outside assistant or organization to implement specific activities and tasks. Your job is not mailing or scheduling or reading or sending e-mail. It's not driving your car or flying on airplanes. Your job is selling. The only way you can sell is to get in front of people.

If you are struggling with how to manage your time more effectively, ask your manager for help. He or she can be a valuable resource, and is often underused. Bring up time management at your next sales meeting and you are likely to find agreement among your colleagues about its importance.

Remember, your time is your money. Spend your time with clients and prospects as if your career depended on it. It does.

EXECUTIVE SUMMARY
For the investor, the currency
for success is money.
For the advisor, the currency
for success is clients.
For the wholesaler, the currency
for success is time.

~18~
What the Boy Scouts Can Teach Us

A myriad of elements completely out of your control — markets, competition, product performance, how your clients feel at any particularly moment — can affect your productivity. But there is one area over which you have a large measure of control: yourself. In particular, you can control the way you prepare for interaction with clients.

Sun Tzu, the ancient Chinese philosopher, knew about preparation and control. "The war is won before the first blow has been struck," is one of his famous sayings, and it is just as applicable to the mental preparation required in wholesaling as it is to warfare. Sun Tzu understood the critical role of questioning in the preparation for winning, saying, "You must learn through planning. You must question the situation." In other words your mental analysis and review of the person you will be meeting with will provide you with the roadmap for victory.

Review your notes before every client interaction. Ask yourself these questions:

1. How much business have I done with this client?
2. Do I need to follow up on anything from prior meetings?
3. What is the potential for future business?
4. What are the priorities of this client?
5. What are the needs, concerns, or objections of this client?
6. What is my objective for this interaction?
7. What is the ideal outcome of this interaction?
8. How can I help this client?
9. Am I prepared with questions that will help me expand the relationship?
10. Am I maintaining a focus on the relationship?

Before you meet with a client or prospect, you must feel confident. Mental preparation is a systematic approach that helps you to feel and exhibit confidence. Do your mental homework before every meeting by asking yourself the above questions. It can make or break your relationship with clients. Sun Tzu knew what he was talking about, then again so did Lord Robert Baden-Powell, the founder of the Boy Scouts. Training, preparation and practice were so important to the Boy Scouts that became enshrined in its motto, Be Prepared! Make that your motto, too.

EXECUTIVE SUMMARY
The war is won before the first blow
has been struck. Be prepared!

~19~
Technology: It's a Means, Not an End

Technology can save you time and help you operate more efficiently. But without your direction and input, technology is powerless to help you achieve your goals. Simply put, technology can't take the place of person-to-person selling.

Think about it. Every sale involves a buying decision. And every buying decision is reached emotionally, then justified logically. It's not surprising, then, that the best wholesalers are emotionally intelligent "people" people, who can direct a client's or prospect's emotions to the desired logical conclusion. Any technology that interposes itself between a wholesaler and the prospect or client, therefore, diminishes personal interaction and reduces the opportunity for selling.

To get the most out of technology ask yourself two questions: How can I use technology to manage my time and territory more effectively? Could the time I'm spending with technology be used to meet face-to-face with an advisor?

E-mails and pocket digital assistants are incredible tools for transmitting data and following up. Cell phones are irreplaceable for turning down time in the car or airport into prime time. PowerPoints and LCD projectors have revolutionized group presentations. But the most effective resource for influencing and persuasion is you, that's your job.

The bottom line is this: Your customers want a real, live, knowledgeable human with whom they can communicate, not a package of silicon chips. Use technology to help you tend to your clients — not as a replacement for heart-to-heart contact.

EXECUTIVE SUMMARY
High tech is invaluable but will never outsell high touch.

~20~
Raise Your Comfort Zone

*M*ost salespeople operate in a comfort zone. If sales fall below a certain level, they get uncomfortable. The discomfort motivates them to make some sales happen. Activity goes up, the business plan is adjusted, and voilà, the sales goal is met. Similarly, if sales are above projections, many salespeople start to coast. They make fewer calls, sales slide, and the process starts all over.

Everyone has a comfort zone. Don't deny it or ignore it. Instead, learn to accept it, manage it, and gradually raise its upper limit, which is what top-producing wholesalers continually seek to do. Raising your comfort zone is a challenge because you must be willing to feel uncomfortable and be willing to change your thinking. The secret is to keep your eye on the prize. Don't depend on a divisional manager to set your sales goals as he or she will never be able to recognize the upper limits of your potential as well as you can. Think big. Then think bigger. You'll expand your comfort zone and surpass any expectations that have been imposed on you.

Don't try to make too big a jump at first. Most people have problems if they double their income in just one year. Fast upswings in income often cannot be sustained or are followed by big dips. Instead, raise your comfort zone gradually by following a long-term plan for continuous improvement. Raise both your lower and upper limits by setting higher minimum tickets and by targeting bigger rep prospects than you considered before.

The only way to get stronger is by pushing yourself out of your current comfort zone into a new, higher one.

EXECUTIVE SUMMARY

World-class wholesalers are willing to endure the discomfort of continually expanding their comfort zone.

~21~
Maximize Your Meetings

Like most wholesalers, you probably have a business plan for the year. But do you create a business plan for each conference you attend? If not, you probably are missing lots of sales opportunities.

Every meeting represents a huge investment. You invest money in registration fees and booth or table displays. You also invest time, especially the valuable time you could be spending with clients. But conferences and meetings provide incredible opportunities and offer huge potential for building relationships. To reap the rewards, you need a concrete plan.

Here's a step-by-step process that will enable you to capitalize on sales opportunities at your next meeting:

1. Find out who will attend the meeting. Create an "A" list of current clients and prospects with you want to initiate or expand relationships. Estimate and write down actual dollar potential for each person.

2. Review the background of each person you will see. What is their business model? Who is their target market? What are their current challenges both professionally and personally? And most important, what can you bring to the table besides your product to help each of them?

3. A week or two before the meeting, arrange appointments with each of those people. Give them a compelling reason to meet with you. Allot the most time to those with the highest potential. Set up as many one-to-one meetings, lunches, and dinners as possible.

4. Confirm all appointments one or two days before the meeting. If anyone cancels, fill the slot with someone else or with some other activity. Your goal is a full agenda.

5. When you attend the program sessions, take notes. Write up a summary on your way home and send it to clients who couldn't attend the meeting. One successful wholesaler I know says his clients really appreciate this service.

Don't waste your time and money attending conferences and meetings without specific objectives. Meetings can be a powerful use of your time if you plan that time wisely.

EXECUTIVE SUMMARY
All successful conferences
have an agenda. Do you?

~22~
You Are the
Search Engine

W hy have Google and other search engines become an essential part of our lives seemingly overnight? Because the Internet is vast, time is at a premium and the ability to find what you want quickly is very valuable. A search engine, therefore, is a great service. So here's how to make yourself an integral and valued part of your clients' business: Become their search engine. Create value in your relationships by positioning yourself as a resource for resources.

You know that continually calling on your clients doesn't work. It simply doesn't make sense is to keep visiting clients, wasting their time with small talk and repitching your products. It's annoying and counterproductive. By contrast, becoming a "search engine" resource will turn you into a guest who's welcomed every time you call on your clients.

Start by creating a series of file folders that you can call Great Resources for Producers. These folders should be topic specific. Your folder titles might look something like this:

Great Resources for Marketing to High-Net-Worth Clients

Great Resources for Seminars

Great Resources for Client Events

Great Resources for Marketing Benefit Plans

Great Resources for Selling Annuities

Great Resources for Generating Referrals

Since you don't target bottom producers, you probably have the opportunity to speak to and learn from some of the most successful producers in the business. Every time you meet with a successful producer, learn what he is doing right. Find out what's really working. It's a funny thing about human nature, even if you were told you had ten minutes for a meeting, if you ask a producer how he got a big new client, he will talk to you for a half hour.

Here's an example of how it might work. Let's say your producer is bringing in significant new business through referrals from accountants. Your producer tells you about how she conducts accounting seminars that can be applied toward continuing education credit. She tells you about a firm she uses that specializes in accounting seminars for professional development that provides a leader's guide and workbooks, does all the paperwork and files for the continuing education credits. This is really, really good stuff for you in your role as a search engine. Capture and record all this value information and be ready to pass it along to a producer who may be ready to implement this seminar strategy.

There's no limit to the types of information and resources you can collect for distribution. Your resource files will fill up with the names of Web sites, articles, books, contacts and coaches. You'll gather information on practice management, sales and marketing, technology, strategies for hiring assistants and so forth.

It's easy to say you are a value-added resource for producers. It's much more difficult to walk your talk. Becoming a search engine is a highly effective way to do that.

Executive Summary

The mind is for thinking. The pen (and computer) are for remembering. Gather, store, manage, and distribute valuable information and you become more valuable to your clients.

The Wholesaler as a Motivator

~23~
Next!

*O*ne of the very real frustrations of wholesaling is rejection. Sales, by its nature, means that many people in the course of a typical day — sometimes even most people — will turn you down, say no or not even pay attention to what you're saying. Maintaining peace of mind and a positive attitude through all this requires tremendous motivation, inner strength and depth of character.

Don't for a minute assume such fortitude is a small thing. Many people would happily leave their job for the freedom, fulfillment and compensation of wholesaling — so long as rejection weren't part of the job. But most people don't have an emotional hide of Teflon, and they can't do what you do.

Senior wholesalers who have been "carrying the bag" for years possess extraordinary strength in handling rejection. In fact, your ability to become a truly great wholesaler will be determined in large measure by your ability to handle rejection. Why? It's really very simple. If you want to sell a lot, you have to ask a lot. And if you ask a lot, you're going to get rejected a lot. Therefore, if you can't handle a lot of rejection, you can't sell a lot. This is true for all wholesalers regardless of experience, skills, or the quality or popularity of their products.

So how do you come to embrace rejection? You don't. The first step in coping with it is realizing that rejection isn't fun, and that some days you just don't want to put up with it. Go ahead and admit it; some days you are just not ready to be turned away.

That's OK. The greatest champions in every field have ebbs and flows of energy and moments of doubt. It's natural, human, and bound to be part of your experience as a wholesaler. The solution is simple: retreat. Not forever, of course, but tactical retreat is a winning strategy that successful armies implement regularly.

It's impossible to renew your strength and revitalize your resolve without retreating. Retreating allows you to connect internally with your inner resources that accept rejection. Like dealing with a difficult personality trait in someone you deeply love, retreating enables you to focus on the rewards of the relationship rather than on its imperfections.

Retreating can take on a number of forms and activities. It's a personal process you must create for yourself. You may wish to take a few minutes to meditate or relax. I like to call a very close friend and engage in a mutually supportive dialogue. That act reinvigorates me.

Retreating might mean just taking a break in the heat of battle to enjoy a hot cup of coffee or a cool ice tea. It could mean a spa day on the weekend or a few spontaneous vacations days with your significant other.

An infinite number of activities can work; it all depends on what connects you to your inner source or center. When it comes to identifying what works for you, the operative guide is the maxim "Know thyself."

The key to handling rejection is threefold. First, be honest and recognize that it presents a challenge. Second, develop and implement a personalized retreat strategy. Third, continually refine and develop your renewal skills.

If you intend to achieve and maintain continuous success as a wholesaler, you must adopt the simple yet powerful mantra: "Next!"

EXECUTIVE SUMMARY

Successful wholesaling requires an incredible expenditure of energy. To maintain momentum and consistent results you must recharge your battery.

~24~
Maintaining Your Motivation for a Lifetime

*I*t's easy to feel pumped after listening to a dynamic speaker at a conference, attending a motivational seminar, reading a great book, or hearing a terrific audio program. These activities succeed in inspiring you and focusing your attention on important business principles.

Unfortunately, the inspiration and the focus don't last. Everyday business dulls the focus while the externally driven inspiration can be superficial and evaporates quickly.

Real motivation and sustained inspiration are internally driven. A booster shot from outside sources can be a plus, but your on-going drivers come from a clear sense of why you do what you do, who you serve, and the benefits of your work. Not sure what that means? Then ask yourself these three questions:

1. What does becoming a great wholesaler mean to you? Obviously, if you lead the pack, you're going to make a whole lot more money. But consider why money is important to you. Money is the medium used to acquire material things such as cars and houses. That, plus the other choices money affords bring the potential for more joy, freedom and security. Most people, of course, want the things that money can buy. But great wholesalers typically are motivated by the fear that they won't have enough money. If anything, they are insecure. The feeling of success that comes with achieving and exceeding goals helps keep insecurity at bay. So instead of denying your insecurity and consequent need for recognition and success, accept those drivers, and use them to motivate yourself.

2. How will achieving greatness as a wholesaler serve your family? Most salespeople want to improve the

lives of their families. Success means being able to share more with loved ones. Giving your family the luxuries associated with success and being generous with close friends and associates brings enormous satisfaction to you and comfort and pleasure to them.

3. How will achieving greatness as a wholesaler serve your clients? Every time you distribute your financial products, your clients make money directly or indirectly, either through a commission or a fee. Assuming your clients offer the right product to the right person at the right time, they make a positive contribution to the lives of others. When properly sold, financial products have a dynamic positive effect on both advisors and their clients.

EXECUTIVE SUMMARY
Motivation is not a matter
of willpower. It's a matter
of want power.

~25~
Achieving
Peak Performance

*A*thletes call it the zone. Artists call it flow. Philosophers refer to the power of now. You may not have a name for it, but you know what it feels like. It's when you're hot, you're on, and you perform at your highest level, easily and effortlessly. As a wholesaler, you know the feeling and you crave it every morning when you go out the door to ply your trade.

It would be great if that feeling could surround every interaction, every selling situation and every presentation. You'd consistently be at your best; better than the rest. While that may not be possible, performing at your peak as much of the time as possible and as consistently as possible is a realistic goal.

The frustrating truth about peak performance, though, is that you can't make it happen through sheer will. It's typically the by-product of creating the proper environment. It's like the steps you take to prepare for sleep — brushing and flossing your teeth, closing the blinds or window shade, turning out the light, fluffing the pillow, adjusting the covers, lying in a certain position and consciously relaxing your body. You set the stage through certain activities and rituals and then you get the desired result: sleep.

Are you surprised, then, when you get on a plane for a cross-country flight and you can't will yourself to sleep for the entire trip? You shouldn't be. No matter how hard you try, falling asleep in that atypical environment, without the benefit of your regular falling-asleep rituals, just won't work. That's why, if you seek consistently high levels of performance, first you must become conscious of the activities or rituals that create the environment for success. I call this your Peak Performance Formula (PPF). What actions and elements create the environment that allows you to maximize your effectiveness? Your PPF might include any number of elements that affect your physical, mental, and emotional well-being. On the physical level, consider diet, exercise, rest, relaxation and alcohol intake. Ignore these elements or fail to make adjustments in them, and your performance is bound to be negatively affected.

On the mental level, set the stage for peak performance by maintaining a positive attitude. Avoid the negative mental input that comes from negative people, books, movies and television. Instead, crowd out negativity by continually programming your mind for success with positive input.

On the emotional level, it is important to be clear and imbued with passion for any activity you engage in. Emotional disturbance will distract you and diminish your performance. Check in on your emotional state. Listen internally and acknowledge how you feel emotionally. Maintain self-awareness and keep your emotions in line, and you will avoid responding inappropriately to the people and situations around you.

Here are just a few elements you might consider including in your PPF:

- Maintain a healthy diet centered around fresh fruits, vegetables and whole grains.
- Avoid eating hotel food whenever possible.
- Adjust your travel schedule to accommodate time for nutritious meals and enough sleep.
- Exercise regularly regardless of your travel schedule.
- Moderate your alcohol intake.
- Read books that inspire you.
- Schedule regular telephone calls or visits with colleagues whom you respect and admire.
- Meditate and calm your mind before every presentation.
- Do not spend time with negative people.
- Spend a few minutes every day reflecting on what you are grateful for in your life.

As a professional wholesaler, your goal must be consistent, high-level performance. Treat yourself like a world-class athlete. The secret to world-class performance is to maintain a world-class regime physically, mentally and emotionally. Use the habits of peak performance to create the environment for peak performance.

Executive Summary

If you owned a million-dollar race horse, would you keep it up all night feeding it beer and pretzels?

~26~
The Purpose of Living Is Living on Purpose

In wholesaling, there is a direct correlation between activity and results. Ultimately, the more qualified producers you create and maintain relationships with, the more money you will make. This attractive equation of activity and financial reward is a source of motivation. In fact, it was probably one of the reasons you decided to pursue a career in wholesaling.

The problem is that it's easy to lose focus and get caught up in the frenetic activity of daily business — meetings with producers, client seminars, phone calls, faxes, e-mails, broker-dealer conferences, expense reports, meetings with your district managers, airplane flights, packing your bags, reading the trade magazines. Well, you get the idea. Our professional satisfaction vanishes when we become overwhelmed with minutia.

For many wholesalers, inner motivation comes from the desire to create a good life for others in addition to themselves. This love and caring for family and others drives the activity. But that is not enough. To stay motivated and avoid spiritual burnout, you need more. That "more" is a connection to a sense of purpose. Real motivation and work satisfaction are possible only when you infuse a deeper meaning into every moment of every day.

All people, regardless of their work, are capable of identifying and maintaining a connection to the greater context in which they function. You needn't be a cancer researcher or Red Cross volunteer in a third-world country to have the connection. It's available to everyone. And I'm sure you meet a few people in the course of the day who either consciously or unconsciously are aware of their connection to purpose. They are the ones who really enjoy what they are doing.

Your statement of purpose, or your mission statement, must contain two key elements: the identification of who you serve and how you serve them. There can be no sense of purpose without service. Your statement of purpose will answer the question, "Why do you do what you do?" And your answer will give you the inner fire to maximize your potential as a wholesaler.

As you write your statement of purpose, don't try to be eloquent or sophisticated. Keep it simple. Focus on how you contribute to the lives of others. Here are a few examples:

- I help investment advisors manifest their clients' retirement dreams.
- I enable financial advisors to annuitize their incomes with fee-based products.
- I assist financial professionals in growing their businesses.
- I provide bank investment reps with resources for improving the lives of older people.

- I help small-business owners attract and retain superior employees.
- I enable affluent clients to transfer their wealth to the people and causes they love instead of to the government.
- I facilitate the creation of legacies.

To summarize: First, give careful thought to your statement of purpose. Then, write it out, memorize it and internalize it. If you make your statement of purpose a living and breathing internal force in your life, you will avoid the spiritual burnout that threatens both your daily productivity and your longevity as a wholesaler. Your statement is your touchstone to peace of mind and fulfillment in the often chaotic world of wholesaling.

EXECUTIVE SUMMARY
*There can be no sense of purpose
without service.*

~27~

Become a
Motivational Speaker

Great wholesalers are much like great motivational speakers. They share magnetism and charisma. They have the power to persuade and inspire. They glow with positive attitude, and above all else, they are extremely effective communicators.

As a wholesaler, you couldn't choose a better role model than a great motivational speaker. Regardless of their subject matter, these speakers inspire you to maximize your potential materially, emotionally, physically, spiritually and mentally. They exude power and win you over by captivating you with stories, jokes and insights. They connect with you emotionally. And when they've finished their talk, you end up saying to yourself, "Yes, I can do it! I should do it! I will do it!" This is the precise effect you should have on the clients and prospects you speak to both one-to-one and in groups.

Motivational speakers are popular because all of us, regardless of our station in life, require inspiration. We crave positive input in a world filled with negativity — and a good old kick in the pants to fulfill our potential. Practically everyone appreciates and feels nourished by a skilled motivational speaker. So imagine how much more popular and more likely to influence others you would be if you became a purveyor of inspiration along with your products.

Your clients want you to perform the role of a motivational speaker, and would love you for doing it. What advisor or producer wouldn't welcome a telephone call or visit from someone they know will shake them out of their lethargy, bring a smile to their face, remind them of what's important, or dispel the loneliness and isolation that often comes with being a financial professional? As a motivational speaker, you will create the empathy that forms the emotional framework of all sales.

When you emulate the skills and traits of a motivational speaker during your presentations, you will notice that your formal presentations become more exciting and effective. Since most wholesaler presentations turn into PowerPoint data dumps, audiences tune out and turn off. If your motivational approach focuses on benefits, you will arouse interest and plant genuine desire among listeners to learn more about your product and how it will benefit them.

Since great motivational speakers are skilled in the art of public speaking, achieving greatness in the area means that you, too, must master platform skills. This means investing time, money and whatever it takes to get really good. Regardless of your current skill level, there is room for you to grow. There always is.

Next time you attend an event with a top-gun motivational speaker, watch the lines form to shake the speaker's hand at the end. It happens every time.

This is what you want, too, isn't it? Become a motivational speaker, and you'll deliver presentations that command attention and open producers' doors.

EXECUTIVE SUMMARY

Speaking is much more about
lighting a fire then filling a bucket.

~28~
The Zen of Wholesaling Mastery

*M*y co-author and I had been signing copies of a recently released sales book. After some time had gone by, he turned to me and said, "Paul, do you realize that in the past hour some of the highest-producing financial professionals in the business, including five past presidents of the Million Dollar Roundtable, have been waiting on line to purchase our book?"

From an egocentric point of view, that was quite flattering. But how could we take credit for the enthusiastic response to a book that nobody had even read?

The response was far more a reflection of the character of the people buying the book than it was of us. These elite professionals truly were peak performers because they were willing to admit they did not know everything — and were excited about learning something new!

The mastery of sales, like the mastery of anything else, is limited only by your openness to the possibility of improvement. This is not about low self-esteem or a poor self-image. Nor does this attitude reflect the virtue of humility. Instead, it's a realization that in order to achieve mastery we must forever remain students.

The open mind is curious, always ready to receive and process new information. The open mind looks forward to new possibilities, strategies and techniques. It understands there is no one way to achieve results in selling. Achieving and maintaining success in wholesaling requires keeping an open mind and being receptive to new ideas and new ways of performing. It's the Zen approach to wholesaling mastery, and here are some simple strategies to master it:

- Attend all sales and marketing sessions when you are working a booth or tabletop exhibit at a conference. Look for retail ideas you can experiment with or apply to your wholesaling efforts. Discuss the core principles with producers to expand your perspective on what was discussed at the sessions.
- Continually participate in professional development workshops. Sales training workshops are great, but you can take many other classes that will also improve your results. Some ideas include a public speaking workshop, a stand-up comedy class to help you add humor to your presentation, a writing class to improve your written communication or a graphics workshop so that you can produce more exciting slide presentations. You might also consider classes to help you become more proficient in areas in which you can help producers, areas such as coaching, direct mail marketing, team building and management.
- Continually ask for feedback. Don't wait for someone to give you unsolicited advice. Ask your

manager, a fellow wholesaler or even one of your clients to critique your presentation. Ask them to write down what they like and don't like about it. If you can manage to put your ego on hold and really listen, you'll be amazed at how much valuable feedback you can get.

- Engage a coach. Coaching has become extremely popular in recent years for a good reason: it works. Working with a coach keeps you in the open mode. A good coach will focus you on what's working and help you to capitalize on your strengths.

- Read books. When you're at the airport, browse the books in the business and personal-growth sections, and find a book that interests you.

- Spend time with colleagues who share your openness for improvement. Most wholesalers develop relationships with a few others. Winners seem to be attracted to winners. These relationships can often have an air of competitiveness, but they also create a fertile environment for new ideas.

- Start teaching what you want to learn. It's amazing how quickly you'll master a sales technique or marketing strategy when you begin sharing it with others.

Maintaining an open mind and devoting time to exploring possibilities for improvement guarantees that you will not only improve your sales results, but also enjoy your job a whole lot more.

EXECUTIVE SUMMARY

The secret to mastery is maintaining the beginner's mind.

~29~
Your Competitive Advantage: Value-First Wholesaling™

*T*he days of value-added wholesaling are rapidly coming to an end. By its very definition, "value-added" implies an afterthought, something added to the sale rather than the basis for doing business.

Value-First Wholesaling, on the other hand, focuses on bringing value to the relationship before you begin to do business. It forms the basis for initiating the relationship. As a value-first wholesaler, you must identify contributions you can bring to the table. The value should be so compelling that the rep will want to meet with you and be eager to do business with you. Give value first, and the sale will follow.

Value-First Wholesaling, a concept I trademarked, follows one of Newton's universal laws of motion: "For every action there is an equal and opposite reaction." In Eastern religious philosophy, it is referred to as karma. The Beatles put it this way: "The love you get is equal to the love you give." On the street, they say, "What goes around comes around."

You will create an impeccable reputation and become a wholesaler everyone wants to do business with if you wake up every morning asking yourself this question: "If I had nothing to sell, what could I do to contribute to the lives of the advisors I will meet with today?"

Value-First Wholesaling is not about providing money for their seminars or marketing materials. It is surely not about golf balls or picking up the tab for dinner and drinks. Helping or showing your appreciation in these ways is fine, of course, but many reps have come to expect such incentives. In fact, responsiveness and great service are also now expected in the mature wholesaling marketplace.

Value-First Wholesaling is about becoming a business-building consultant. It's about becoming a coach. It's about becoming a practice management consultant who provides valuable strategies and techniques. It's about becoming a strategic partner with prospects *before* they become clients and continuing to help them build their business after they become clients.

Value-First Wholesaling is not about getting bigger market share of your clients' books; it's about helping to make your clients' books bigger. Don't worry, you'll get the business. It's a universal law.

EXECUTIVE SUMMARY

Open with, "I can help you grow and manage your business more effectively," and you'll never have a problem closing.

~30~
Elect Yourself to the Hall of Fame

Consider the difference between wholesalers who never quite make it and those who achieve greatness. The truth is, very little separates the also-rans from the Hall of Famers. It's all a matter of numbers.

Take baseball, and say a player is up at bat 20 times a week. For a mediocre player batting .200, that translates into four hits a week. Not quite Hall of Fame performance. But just one more hit per week would translate into a .250 batting average — perhaps enough to qualify for the Cooperstown honor. Isn't it fascinating how such a minor improvement can result in such major change?

It's the same story in wholesaling. By adding just one more sales call per day, or one more seminar a week or one more client event a month, your overall production level can increase significantly. Your path to break-out levels of success depends on consistently implementing this strategy of "one more." Focus on implementing the "one more" activities that that will make you eligible for the Hall of Fame.

EXECUTIVE SUMMARY
*Which "one more" strategy will get
you into the Hall of Fame?*

The Wholesaler as Communicator and Presenter

~31~
Are You Dressing for Success?

Years ago I had the privilege of attending a presentation by John Malloy, author of the business classic *Dress for Success*. During his talk, Malloy asked the audience to identify the color of his suit. The suit was dark, and audience members shouted out a variety of answers: blue, navy blue, grey, dark grey, black, blue-grey. Malloy told us we were all wrong. The color of his suit, he said, was green — the color of money. Malloy went on to explain the importance of appearance and selecting the right business clothes, saying that we should not base what we wear on what is fashionable or what we enjoy, but rather on what is most likely to result in business success.

Malloy's point is as valid today as it was then. Put aside your vanity and other criteria for making appearance decisions and allow your desire to produce sales be your guide in determining what you wear and how you look. Dress for results. Before you go out the door in the morning, make sure you look like a champion.

Here are some guidelines, strategies and tips.

- Take the time to perfect your wardrobe. To achieve results, it may be worth hiring an image consultant. Search the Internet and you are sure to find a local consultant who will help you for a small fee. Image consultants will help you perfect the most effective business look for you, including the selection of your best colors and styles. Many will even shop with you. If a consultant isn't for you, go to one of the better department or specialty stores (Nordstrom, Saks and Brooks Brothers are good choices), which usually have experienced salespeople who can guide you. In either case, inform the person helping you that you work in sales in the financial industry.

- Use the IBM look as your guide. One of today's great business stories is IBM. They built one of the most successful businesses in history on a philosophy of sales and service. The IBM sales culture has always had a "look." The look is simple: a navy blue suit, white shirt and usually a red tie. While there is more choice today, that combination is a wonderful standard and guide. Women, of course, have more latitude in dress, but the same conservative principles apply.

- Wear the best wardrobe you can afford. In the long run, fine clothes are lot less expensive than cheap clothes. A $1,000 suit will last five or ten times longer than a $200 suit. You will also convey to your clients the subliminal message that you are successful — and everyone wants to do business with successful people.

- Dress equal to or slightly better than your clients. If you want to have top producers as your clients, you must look as good as or better than they do.

- Don't worry about being boring. Fine business clothes are by nature designed to enhance you like a properly chosen frame of a picture. Clothes constructed out of excellent materials, styled for business, that are expertly tailored will bring home the business more effectively than flashy clothes. If you want to add a dash of flash, you can do that by your choice of tie, handkerchief or scarf.

- Wear natural fabrics. Most synthetic fibers look cheap compared real wool, silk, and cotton.

- Regularly examine and assess your clothes. As soon as a collar or cuff is starting to show wear, throw it away. Nothing screams failure as loud as worn clothes.

- Choose your accessories carefully. There's nothing wrong with wearing a fine watch or, if you are a woman, a tasteful brooch. Accessories can enhance your overall appearance. The problem arises when accessories and jewelry divert attention from you. Jewelry that is oversized, dangles or exudes too much glitter should be avoided. In other words, no bling.

- Business casual should be just that: casual, not sloppy. An event billed as business causal doesn't mean come as you like. The operative word is "business." Evening events require dark pressed slacks, dark jacket and shoes and an open-collar shirt for men. For women, it's the equivalent relaxed business look. The "golf look" is perfect for both men and women at daytime business casual events. Sweaters are also a wonderful staple for business casual.

- Select and prepare your clothing the night before work or an event. Whenever possible, pick out the clothes you will wear before you go to sleep and have them ready to pack or put on in the morning. Preparing the night ahead gives you plenty of time to assemble the right combination and give your shirt or blouse a quick iron or your shoes a little buffing, if necessary. The next morning you can dress calmly and not worry about your attire.

- Pay attention to grooming. No matter how hectic your schedule or how tired you feel, don't compromise your personal appearance for any reason at anytime. If you are a man and have a heavy beard, you might need to carry an electric razor to clean up for that evening seminar or client event. It's best not to have a mustache or beard. Research has shown that it can produce a negative response in business. If you chose to have facial hair, be sure to keep it impeccably trimmed at all times. It goes without saying teeth and nails should be immaculately clean at all times. Keep a toothbrush and floss on your bag.

- Eliminate all bad hair days. Don't put off that haircut when you need it. Keep your hair under control and groomed throughout the day. Long hair and trendy haircuts are fine if you are a rock musician or produce independent films; they have no place in the world of wholesaling. Conservative hair lengths and styles only please.

Your clothing and grooming are the silent, subconscious communicators that tell everyone who you are and what you are about. Be flawless in your appearance and you will not only communicate success, you will attract it.

EXECUTIVE SUMMARY

How you look constitutes 55 percent of what you communicate. When you are face-to-face with a prospect what does your appearance say?

~32~
The U-Conversation

Here's a simple, effective format for talking to clients. It's called the U-conversation.

Start light. Engage in a friendly, topical discussion. Talk about things of interest to the client, such as their golf game, their kids, a favorite team or the trip they just took. Make rapport your prime objective.

Next, direct the conversation to business. Discuss how they have been doing, their current needs and concerns, and how you can help them. Thank them for any business they have written, and discuss any possibilities coming up.

Finally, before you leave, return the conversation to more personal topics. In other words, make a U-turn. Ask them about their outside interests or their plans for the weekend. Lighten it up once again, and end on a happy note.

Make the U-conversation your format. With it, you engage clients and prospects emotionally, accomplish the business purpose of your meetings, and leave on a pleasant personal level that motivates clients to want to see you again.

The U-conversation provides a great way to manage the time you spend with each client. And it's a pleasant way for you to do business. Wholesaling should be fun and enjoyable. If it's not, you will either burn out or lose interest.

Of course, the U-conversation works only if you are sincere, conduct truly relevant conversations, listen carefully, and take a real interest in the personal lives of your clients. Make the process mechanical and you will repel rather than attract clients.

EXECUTIVE SUMMARY

Remember to keep the "U" conversation focused on them and not "U."

~33~
Hypnotize Them

Old sales pros used to say, "Whatever they do, you do." They didn't know it, but they were using techniques of today's neurolinguistic programming, which involves communicating with people in their own style and manner.

Before you can persuade people, you must meet them on their own frequency. Find it by listening and observing the visual, vocal, and verbal communication style and patterns of the person to whom you are speaking. Then mirror the style.

Visual elements include dress, grooming, posture, gestures, eye contact and facial expression. Vocal elements are tone of voice, volume, rate of speed and clarity. The verbal element consists of the words being used. Your message and call to action are much more likely to be heard and acted upon if you match as many of your communication elements as possible with the person you are speaking with.

EXECUTIVE SUMMARY
People like and trust people
who are like themselves.

~34~
It's Not About You

*E*arly in my career as roadman for a leading management consulting firm, I was assigned to deliver a two-day training program to a prestigious Wall Street firm. Unsure of myself as a trainer and intimidated by the top-producing stockbrokers who would be participating, I approached the assignment with trepidation.

Late in the afternoon of the second day, I phoned in to the head office and asked for Ned, my manager, coach and mentor. He asked how the program went and I responded with enthusiasm and a new level of self-confidence: "They loved me!"

Ned responded with two words that I now realize shaped my entire career as a trainer, speaker, and consultant: "Who cares?" Talk about instant ego deflation. But because I knew Ned was on my side and that only good intentions were behind his words, I reacted with minimal defensiveness. Still, I wasn't sure what he meant.

Ned explained that the success of my effort could not and should not be measured by how it felt to me. Similarly, success should not be measured by how much the audience liked me. The success of any presentation can only be measured in relation to the desired outcome. In other words, did the audience do what you wanted it to do?

Think about your own presentations. As a result of your remarks, what would you like your audience to believe, do, or say? What would you like to have happen at the end of your presentation? Do you have a clear and precise call to action? Only by having a clear idea of what you want your audience to do after they hear your talk — and then measuring the results — do you know whether your presentation has been a success.

For example, if you are presenting to a group of 200 advisors at a broker-dealer conference, you might want 10 or 20 advisors to request more information. If you are presenting a sales tip at a lunch-and-learn meeting, for instance, your goal might be to position yourself as a valued resource to a few advisors whom you have targeted as good prospects.

Sometimes your role is simply to educate or transfer information, such as when you deliver a CE program. While delivering Continuing Education Credits is one measurable outcome, initiating and growing relationships is worthy of consideration too.

Unless your goal is purely to entertain, which is rarely the case, measuring your presentation by applause or laughter is a mistake. Although these are wonderful and laudable features of highly effective presentations, they are hardly true measures of your effectiveness.

Ned's two words — "Who cares?" — remind us that wholesaling is not about satisfying the speaker's emotional needs. Attention, accolades and applause are nice, but don't let them divert you from your mission.

EXECUTIVE SUMMARY

Your presentations are not the place to get your emotional needs met. They're about achieving results!

~35~
Design the Perfect Presentation in Five Minutes

Here's an elegant way to conceive and design a presentation easily and effortlessly. I call it the Modular Design Approach (MDA). It's based on breaking down every presentation, regardless of length, into mini-presentations or modules, each of which has a beginning, middle, and end.

MDA makes presenting easier because it allows you to design and deliver your presentation in small bite-size pieces. This modular focus prevents you from becoming overwhelmed, and allows you to change the order of the modules as you fine-tune the flow of your presentation. By adding or deleting a module, you can extend or shorten your presentation. MDA provides natural points at which to take breaks, solicit feedback or questions, and make a transition to a new idea.

Here's how it works. Let's assume the purpose of your program is to introduce your fee-based product to a group of independent financial advisors, and your desired outcome is to set up individual appointments with qualified advisors after your presentation. Depending on your audience and their level of sophistication, your modules might be:

Module 1. Introduction to the Presentation

Module 2. The Benefits of Selling a Fee-Based Product

Module 3. How to Make the Transition to a Fee-Based Business Model

Module 4. How to Present the Fee-Based Investment Solution

Module 5. How Your Organization Manages Money

Module 6. Call to Action

The six modules could represent a one-hour breakout presentation at an annual broker-dealer meeting. It's easy to see how you could use one or two of these modules for a twenty-minute presentation at lunch.

The third step is to design the modules themselves. The modules use the same three-element structure as the program itself: introduction, body and conclusion. As the old-timers used to say: tell 'em what you're gonna tell 'em; tell 'em; and then tell 'em what you told 'em.

The introduction describes what the module is all about, its purpose, its importance and the benefits of listening to the body of the module. The introduction should sell what is to follow.

The body or content of the module usually consists of one to three points or elements that are the payload. The body delivers what you promised in the introduction. Take Module 2, for example, The Benefits of Selling a Fee-Based Product. The main points might be: 1. Annuitize your book of business; 2. Offer a product that appeals to the affluent; 3. Spend less time on maintenance with fee-based products.

The content of a perfect module should support the purpose of your presentation and yet, with minimal adjustments, have enough integrity to stand by itself. Using the sales process as an analogy, if the introduction delivers the benefits, the body or content of the module gives the features.

The conclusion of the module reviews the benefits, the main points and how they relate to your main point. The biggest difference between the conclusion of a module and the conclusion of your presentation is that the conclusion of your presentation will deliver an ultimate call to action, a close. If you are delivering an individual module as a short presentation, you will probably have to add the call to action.

Modular Design Approach gives you a solid framework for any presentation you might deliver. Think modular, design modular, and deliver modular. MDA will take the stress out of the design process and enable you to design any presentation in a matter of minutes.

EXECUTIVE SUMMARY
A presentation is much easier for you to create and for your audience to swallow when it's broken up into bite-size pieces.

~36~

The Hour of Presentation Power

*L*et me share a secret of first-class presenters: one hour of on-site preparation right before a scheduled talk.

Just as athletes get to their sports venue hours before a game to warm up and prepare, and actors arrive at a theater early to put on their makeup and go over their lines, great presenters leave nothing about their presentations to chance. They arrive at least one hour before their event to prepare themselves emotionally, check the room logistics and set the stage for a peak performance.

Want to be at your peak when presenting your ideas to a group? Here's a to-do list that will transform the 60 minutes before your next presentation into an hour of power:

1. Take ownership of your presentation space. The area you will speak from is your stage, and that makes it very special. Spend five or ten minutes familiarizing yourself with the area. Walk around and visualize yourself presenting. Locate the optimum spots for speaking. Set up your notes and materials for easy access.

2. Rearrange the furniture, if necessary. Most meeting rooms routinely have a huge aisle in the center, wasting prime real estate. If possible, make the aisles off-center, or close up the center aisle as much as possible. If the speaking area is cluttered or in any other way is set up so that the focus is not on you, rearrange it. Remove unnecessary tables or chairs. Be sure you have enough clear space in the front of the room.

3. Test the audiovisual equipment. Do a microphone sound-check, making sure the room has no dead

spots or areas that generate feedback. If you will be using a laptop and LCD projector that aren't yours, test the remote slide advance and other features. Make sure you're comfortable with the equipment and that an audio-visual person will be present at the start of your presentation should anything go wrong.

4. Remove seats. Most rooms are set with too many seats. For a large event without a confirmed guest list, it's usually safe to remove about 10 percent of the chairs. A full house always looks better. You can bring in more chairs later if you need them. If possible, remove chairs from the front few rows. When audience members have a choice of seating, they rarely fill up the front.

5. Focus your intentions. Assume success. Ask yourself, "What do I want the audience to learn or feel?" Spend time before every presentation assessing the needs of your client and the audience. Every presentation should deliver value. Focus on the value you will bring to your audience. Spend five or ten

minutes to focus your intentions on your professional mission, your presentation, and the value you will offer the audience.

6. Make sure you have a hard copy of the presentation with you, in case all the technology fails and you have to refer to your notes. It's helpful if the presentation is printed in large type (20 points or larger) and is double spaced.

If you want to gain recognition as a commanding speaker, arrive early and set the stage for success. Dynamic presentations begin before you get up to speak; they begin with the hour of power.

EXECUTIVE SUMMARY
Prepare for your presentation as if your professional success depended upon it. Because it does!

~37~
You Deserve a
Fantastic Introduction

*E*ver notice how movie trailers do a great job of interesting you in an upcoming film? "Wow," you think to yourself, "I've got to see that movie, it looks great!" The trailer has programmed you for the movie, and you are predisposed to enjoy it. That's exactly what a good introduction accomplishes for a speaker. In fact, a good introduction is so important, you should never let anyone other than yourself prepare your own introduction.

Invest an hour or two in writing an introduction that can be read by others. Your introduction should answer two questions: Who the heck are you? Why should I listen to you? It should be no more than one minute long, and it should be conversational. It should reflect your style. If you are an entertaining presenter, your introduction might include humor. If your style is more direct, your introduction should be straightforward.

Answer the question about who are you with information relevant to your audience. This includes any or all of the following:

- Current position and responsibilities
- Size and focus of your organization
- Length of service in the financial industry
- Positions held in the past
- Past experience of value in your present role
- Professional designations, such as CFP
- Relevant academic degrees, such as an MBA or a master's degree in economics
- Membership or involvement with trade organizations, such as Financial Planning Association or National Association of Insurance and Financial Advisors

- Media recognition, such as published articles and radio or television appearances
- Honors or other recognition received

The mentions should be brief and story-like in their narration. The answer to the second question — about why people should listen to you — should be customized to your audience. For an audience of financial professionals, the introduction should describe the broad nature of your work in terms of how you serve their needs and help them build or manage their business. It should address how you help them create a better life for themselves and the specialized services you offer that set you apart from other wholesalers with similar products.

An introduction for producers' clients should present you as a representative of a financial organization rather than as a salesperson. It's OK to position yourself as a communicator of general investment information, news, and market trends based on the research of your organization, but avoid implying that you posses the expertise of a portfolio manager. Position yourself as a member of an extraordinary team of professionals dedicated to making positive contributions to clients' financial lives.

An effective introduction will cause the audience to have a positive mindset for your presentation. It will position you as a credible person who has important and relevant information to impart. Your introduction will maximize the way both you and your message are received.

EXECUTIVE SUMMARY

Your audience is always tuned in radio station WII-FM —What's In It For Me? Your introduction should answer this question.

~38~
The Mike Will Set You Free

*T*oo many wholesalers misuse or fail to use one of the most valuable audiovisual aids at their disposal: the microphone. Even if you have a powerful voice and great stage presence, a microphone adds a dimension to your presentation that will make you seem larger and more important — especially to those seated at the back or the sides of the room. While using a mike for a roundtable talk to eight or ten people is unnecessary (and to so small a group using one would seem downright odd), amplifying your voice for an audience of 25 or more people is not only appropriate, it's effective and even welcome.

Consider your audience. Many times, if you are addressing financial advisors and their clients, baby boomers will be the youngest ones in the room. They and the older members of the audience will be delighted if you use a mike because they otherwise might have trouble hearing you — and the last thing they would admit is that they are missing much of what you are saying.

So go ahead and use a mike. The best one for wholesaler presentations is a wireless lavaliere. It consists of a tiny microphone that is clipped onto your jacket lapel, dress or shirt front, plus a small transmitter the size of a pack of cigarettes that the audio-visual person working the system attaches to your belt or places in a pocket. The mike is wired to the transmitter that sends a signal to the sound equipment. Since the mike isn't wired to a podium, you have the freedom to walk around and work all areas of the stage and the audience. It's a very common device, but unless you request it in advance, you may be given the standard podium mike.

Before your talk, test your mike. Make sure the volume is correct for the room. Practically every mike setup can be adjusted. If your voice sounds tinny, ask the audio-visual attendant to adjust the mike to give your voice "bottom." You should sound like yourself, only fuller and with slightly greater volume. When you start your presentation, ask those in the room if the sound is comfortable and whether they can hear you, regardless of where they are seated. Since your message is so important, isn't it worth a little effort to make sure your audience hears it?

EXECUTIVE SUMMARY
There's no substitute for content and talent, but your microphone can significantly enhance both.

~39~
Using a
Podium

G et rid of it. It's a barrier between you and your audience. Its only real value: a place to hold your water glass.

~40~
Presence: What Every Audience Really Wants

Wholesaler presentations can take the form of a lunch meeting at a wirehouse, a cluster of meetings for independent financial advisors, breakout sessions at an annual broker-dealer meeting, a panel at a top-producer conference, a continuing education program or a client-referral workshop at a restaurant or hotel. No matter the setting, your audience just wants one thing: You.

In this age of 'round-the-clock media, the one thing people want to see when a real live person comes to address them is...a real live person! If they wanted data, they would have gone on the Internet, read a book, listened to a CD, or scanned a brochure. They don't want a data dump, they want a connection.

Think about a presenter you consider exceptional. What's the attraction? Is it what he says or how he says it? Is it the information or how he makes you feel? You know the answer. If you want to connect with your audience, you need to give them something to like. You've got to give them you. You've got to show up on a deeper level, which is called presence.

Presence cannot be contrived. By its very definition, it is not a manipulative technique used to produce specific emotional responses. In fact, it is just the opposite. The quality of presence is not created by doing but by being. Because it is not technique, the element of presence is easy to write off as something New Age-y or touchy-feely. It's easier to accept if you think of it as a powerful and invisible force. Other such forces include magnetism, electricity and, on a human level, love. They cannot be seen, but they affect practically every aspect of our daily living.

When you bring more of your own presence to the presentation, your audience experiences a deeper relationship with you. Audiences often describe this experience as authenticity. When you are authentic, your audience knows it and they appreciate it. They connect because there is more of a "someone" in the room to connect to.

The secret to giving of yourself in public is to conduct a "Presence Scan" before every presentation. The Presence Scan is the most powerful presentation technique you can employ to maximize your effectiveness. Here's how to do it.

Close your eyes and begin with a physical review of your body. Direct your consciousness to each part of your body, beginning at your feet. Continue upward, allowing yourself to "be" with each part of your body for a few moments until you get to your head.

Next, direct your attention to your heart and affirm your intention to serve your audience with a presentation that will help them in their businesses and their lives. This affirmation will project you as a strategic partner with your audience, which is the opposite of appearing as a self-serving salesperson.

Finally, create and maintain a positive image of your audience and their willingness to accept your intention to serve them. Silently communicate your good intentions and your desire to work together to everyone's advantage.

With these steps behind you, when you begin your presentation, the real you will be up there in front of the audience, presenting with presence and authenticity.

EXECUTIVE SUMMARY

Give your audience the present of your presence. There's no substitute for authenticity.

~41~
Knock 'em Out
Like Ali

One of my personal heroes is Muhammad Ali. Many sports writers and authorities rank him not only as the greatest boxer of all time but as one of history's greatest athletes. For me, his incredible physical skill is exceeded only by the quality of his heart and mind.

During his peak years as a competitor, Ali was banned from boxing for his political beliefs. Instead of becoming bitter, he accepted what he was powerless to control and maintained faith in his position. Ali patiently waited, without malice, until his license to box was reinstated. When he finally received permission to return to the ring, Ali was no longer in his prime physically, and he had to depend on his superior intelligence to defeat some incredibly worthy opponents. He combined his positive mental attitude — exemplified in his often repeated affirmation, "I am the Greatest" — with his equally effective tactical skills.

Perhaps the most important tactic Ali employed was his trademark "rope-a-dope." Ali knew that the knockout power that served him well in his youth had waned. Now he was regularly fighting younger and, in many cases, stronger opponents. He needed a strategy that would give him the opportunity to win these later fights by the judges' decisions, and rope-a-dope was the answer.

Ali would come out at the opening bell of each round with a flurry of excitement. He would throw multiple combinations with incredible speed. He would dance around, bobbing and weaving the like the butterfly he was a decade earlier. The crowds would roar at his magnificence, speed, grace and power.

After a minute or less, Ali would lean against the ropes, protecting his face and head with his hands, and let his opponent hammer his arms and parts of his body that could absorb punishment with very little damaging effect. Finally, toward the last seconds of each round, when his opponent was tired, Ali would bounce off the ropes and once again build up points by peppering his opponent.

Ali knew the importance of the beginning and end of each round. He succeeded in impressing both the spectators and the judges. It's hard to determine exactly how many rounds or fights were decided by the perception of superiority created by the rope-a-dope tactic, but it's safe to say that it played a significant role.

The big opening and big close proved to be a winning strategy for Ali. Let it be a winning strategy for you, too, every time you deliver a presentation. Begin every presentation with energy and liveliness. Your opening will implant a first impression that will affect the audience's perception and reception of what follows.

Your close is equally important. Regardless of how terrific your presentation is, it's easy for the audience to remember it as mediocre if your close fails to keep them engaged and involved. Restate and reinforce your message in a compelling and emotionally charged way. You'll earn the respect of your audience, and you'll be more likely to achieve the results you want.

Craft your opening and closing carefully. Your audience does not necessarily appreciate your need to "get warmed up." They do appreciate the professionalism you display when your opening is well crafted. Similarly, your ending should not simply taper off like a balloon losing air. Your ending should be as well designed and delivered as your opening. It's truly the punch line to your remarks.

If you want to be a champion presenter, come out swinging and deliver big at the end, just like Ali.

EXECUTIVE SUMMARY
Craft and deliver a big opening and a big close and you'll knock'em out like Muhammed Ali.

~42~
Slides Tell;
You Sell

Far be it from me to criticize PowerPoint, Micro-
soft's ubiquitous presentation software. But one
common flaw in wholesaler presentations — and in
the presentations of almost everyone else, too — is
over-reliance on slides. The power of any presentation
is in the emotional connection generated between the
speaker and the audience. Slides and their higher-tech
equivalents provide logical support and evidence, not
emotion. If slides could sell, your company would be
e-mailing PowerPoint presentations to all your clients and you would be out of a job.

That said, slides do convey important data and concepts that influence the decision-making process of your audience. In a sense, you, the wholesaler are doing the emotional selling while your slides are delivering the factual information that furnishes the rationale for the sale. To do that, your slides must be positioned properly.

Here's how to make sure your slides support your sales message:

- Screen placement. The screen should not be in the center of the stage. Instead, place it to the far right or to the far left of the stage and angled toward the center. If the screen is in the center of the stage, directly behind you, you will probably walk in front of it at times and your shadow will distract the audience. Also, you are the main attraction and the star. You — not slides — should own the prime center real estate.

- Lighting. Keep the lights that beam on you as bright as possible. Your power to influence and create a relationship with the audience is drastically diminished when you stand in the dark. To optimize your lighting, design your slides for a well-lit environment. Choose colors, font size, font style, and content that work well in well-lit rooms (white or bright yellow letters on a dark background). Use a projector with a high lumen output. The brighter the projector, the brighter you can turn up the lights. Finally, make adjustments in the existing room lighting. Shut off or, if necessary, unscrew bulbs or remove lights that shine directly across the room. If possible, use a rear-screen projector.

- Create speaker-driven presentations. Use a minimalist approach to slides. Chances are that if the marketing department provided you with the slides, they are dense with stats, data and product information. This is the marketing department's area of expertise. Your area of expertise should be initiating, developing and maintaining mutually profitable relationships. Keep your slide content as simple as possible. Also, avoid data slides that are difficult to read. They frustrate your audience and create negativity.

As a wholesaler, your objective in any presentation is to generate a positive emotional response to you and to your products. Your slides, properly used, are powerful tools that can support your ideas, justify your logic, reinforce your argument, endorse your proposal or restate a point. But used ineffectively, they result in lost wholesaling opportunities.

Here is a simple test to determine if you use slides effectively. Would your relationship with your audience improve if you were *un*able to use slides at your presentation? If you answered yes or maybe, then reexamine the way you use your slide show. Just remember: slides don't sell; you do.

EXECUTIVE SUMMARY
If your audience is more interested
in your slides than you,
you're in big trouble.

~43~
Sweat the Small Stuff

Too many wholesaler presentations fail because seemingly small, but important, logistical details have been overlooked. You can lose audience attention and fail to accomplish your presentation objective if you overlook the staging elements that are unique to your venue, whether it's a lunchroom, boardroom, office conference room, hotel conference room, restaurant or auditorium. Here are three staging elements to control:

Food and alcohol. Never make a presentation while food is being served or eaten. Audiences cannot give you their complete attention while they are eating or while servers are wandering around the room. It is far better to have 100 percent of the audience's attention for 20 minutes than 50 percent for 40 minutes. Plan to present before or after, but never during, meal service. If your speaking time is limited, ask the maitre d' to have the desserts on the table before the meal and have pots of coffee and pitchers of water placed on each table.

Alcohol may be an even bigger distraction. It is a powerful depressant to the central nervous system, diminishing the ability of your audience to pay attention and listen. Ideally, you should eliminate alcohol from the event and provide it only on request. Sometimes it is unavoidable, such as at client seminars. In these cases, minimize the effect of alcohol by having it served after you have completed your presentation.

Room temperature. Room temperature can make or break your presentation. It's usually not as big a problem in office buildings as it is in hotel conference rooms, where it's usually too warm. When meeting room temperature rises above 72 degrees, people tend to get drowsy and may actually fall asleep. The ideal temperature for a meeting room is 68 to 70 degrees. Because it's impossible to make the temperature ideal for everybody in the room, concentrate on keeping it cool enough to hold your listeners' attention.

Seating arrangements. Seating is another common logistical pitfall. Rarely do service attendants configure your meeting room correctly. If the room is set with round tables, I've found it best to remove all seats that put people's backs toward the speaker's podium or presentation area. If seats are arranged in auditorium fashion, eliminate the center aisle when possible. The center is prime real estate. Put your aisles off to the right and left. Instead of putting chairs or tables in parallel rows, use a herringbone configuration with the seats angled toward the center of the room. If space allows, give people breathing room. Separate the chairs by six inches to a foot, and separate rows by a couple of feet.

Like a professional actor, you must take control of the staging of your presentation. Whether it's the temperature, food or seating, logistics can have a major impact on your success as a presenter.

EXECUTIVE SUMMARY
Elephants don't bite.
Mosquitoes do.

~44~
Become a Seminar Guru
(and a Magnet to Top Producers)

*I*f you want to become a magnet for top-producing reps and rising stars — and watch your sales explode — establish yourself as the guru of seminars and client events. This is one of the most worthwhile strategies for adding value to your relationships. Reps who are attracted to seminar selling and client events are the kinds of reps you want as clients. They are motivated and willing to take action to build their business. Top producers are attracted to seminars and client events, and top producers will be attracted to you as the guru.

Many producers seek sponsorship for their events, and this can open lots of doors. But if you want to set yourself above the great sea of wholesalers, you need to bring something else to the table: expertise. Most wholesalers can contribute sponsorship to some degree, but how many can contribute advice and consult on how to improve event results?

Becoming a seminar guru is also the fast track to developing your own professional skills in this area. While conducting seminars and events continues to be one of the core competencies of wholesaling, many wholesalers, unfortunately, aren't very competent in these areas. It's not because they don't have ability, it's because they continually make the same mistakes and reinforce practice habits rather than break through from good to great. Teaching others how to conduct seminars and events will improve your own skills in these areas and give you confidence.

Providing advisors with sound seminar selling training and coaching has proven to be one of the most effective strategies for creating enduring wholesaling success.

EXECUTIVE SUMMARY
Position yourself as a seminar guru and you'll attract advisors like a magnet.

Epilogue

Somewhere down the road, you will retire from your professional life. While your daily work may end, your story will continue. It will continue in the form of a social legacy that continues to shape the lives of the people you touched and influenced during your working years.

Long after the records vanish of how many times you and your team made or surpassed your sales targets, your influence in the lives of those with whom you interacted will live on. The advisors and team members you have served and worked with will remember not only how you have helped them, but how you made them feel.

Seize the opportunity to empathize, support and inspire. Seek to add value in every relationship. That way, you will master not only wholesaling, but life.

About Paul Karasik

Paul Karasik is one of the leading consultants in the financial industry. Paul has devoted 18 years helping financial professionals achieve their goals. He is President of The Wholesaler Institute, a sales and management training and consulting organization dedicated to increasing financial product sales.

Paul is also President of The Business Institute, which helps insurance professionals and financial advisors sell and market their products and services more effectively. He is the author of seven books, including *22 Keys to Sales Success: How to Make It Big in Financial*

Services, co-authored with Jim Benson; *How to Market to High-Net-Worth Households; Seminar Selling; How to Make It Big in the Seminar Business;* and *Sweet Persuasion.*

His articles appear regularly in leading financial industry publications including Registered Rep, National Underwriter, On Wall Street, Investment, Investment Advisor and Financial Planning. Paul is the Founder of the American Seminar Leaders Association and is a frequent keynote speaker at top producer meetings and conferences including Million Dollar Round Table.

About The Wholesaler Institute

Increasing sales is your goal.
Developing a world-class wholesaling
team is ours.

Our business is the art and science of wholesaling. As the leader in wholesaler training and selling systems, we offer customized training and systems to meet the specific needs of your wholesaling team. With The Wholesaler Institute, your sales team will learn how to:

- Maximize sales of financial products
- Maintain a competitive advantage in all market conditions

- Stand out in the crowded financial marketplace
- Reposition themselves from product pushers to strategic marketing partners

If your organization would like to sell more mutual funds, securities, insurance products, managed accounts, annuities, or any other financial product, we can help. We can improve the performance of your:

- Regional wholesalers
- Divisional managers
- Key accounts managers
- Inside sales teams
- Inside sales managers
- National sales managers

What does The Wholesaler Institute do?

Through training and consulting, we help financial product manufacturers achieve their sales goals. We address your precise needs and desired outcomes by customizing all of our training, coaching, management consulting services, and value-added programs to fit your organization.

What services do we offer?

- Sales training for all members of your sales team
- Presentation skills training
- Writing, design, and production of value-added presentations
- Training for the trainer of value-added programs
- Comprehensive coaching programs

How can you get started?

Book Paul Karasik, president of The Wholesaler Institute, to present a pilot program at an upcoming national, divisional or regional sales meeting. This program gives your wholesaling team valuable professional development and infuses your meeting with an added sense of passion, purpose and commitment. Presentations include:

- Mastering the Art and Science of Wholesaling™
- Closing More Sales From the Inside™
- How to Deliver a Dynamic Wholesaler Presentation™
- Conducting Perfect Seminars and Client Events™
- Maximizing Leadership Effectiveness™

Call toll-free 866-473-7600 for your FREE Wholesaler Institute CD or to find out how your organization can achieve your sales goals with our customized training and consulting. Visit our Website: *www.wholesalerinstitute.com.*

Subscribe to our FREE e-newsletter
The Wholesaler Minute

Supercharge your sales with our bi-monthly newsletter The Wholesaler Minute.

Each issue will provide you with proven wholesaling strategies and techniques, sales ideas you can take to your clients as well as personal motivation.

To subscribe go to: *www.wholesalerinstitute.com* or call toll free 866-473-7600

More Books By Paul Karasik

■ **22 Keys to Sales Success: How to Make It Big in Financial Services**

This book, co-authored with James Benson, will change your life. Learn the best practices of the highest-producing financial services professionals and you are guaranteed to exceed all of your sales goals. Regardless of your experience level in the business, each key will unlock a new door on your path to sales success, with proven, actionable strategies and techniques. The keys include powerful scripts, checklists, quizzes, and lots more. It is a must read for every financial professional!

Published by Bloomberg Press, 199 pages, hardcover

■ How to Market to High-Net-Worth Households: Attracting Affluent Clients with Client Events

Follow this easy-to-implement plan and you will create a steady stream of qualified affluent prospects, gather additional assets from your ideal clients, and attract new referral business quickly and easily. This book delivers proven step-by-step strategies and techniques, telephone scripts that are guaranteed to achieve results, powerful marketing letters, checklists for organizing your business procedures, exercises for designing your business plan, and much, much more.

Published by The Business Institute, 160 pages, hardcover

■ **Seminar Selling: The Ultimate Resource Guide for Marketing Financial Services**

This comprehensive guide is written for financial services professionals who want to attract motivated clients, increase sales, expand their client base (quickly), and make more money. You will learn how to fill seats at your seminar, design a flawless financial seminar, deliver a seminar that will attract motivated clients, tap into hidden financial seminar markets, and how to motivate prospects to take action with you. This how-to manual includes hundreds of essential contacts.

Published by McGraw-Hill, 238 pages, hardcover

■ Sweet Persuasion: The Illustrated Guide to Closing the Sale

When you apply the simple and yet powerful strategies of *Sweet Persuasion*, selling becomes a creative process that feels good. You will learn how to close the sale when you open it, how to eliminate objections, how to get and stay motivated, and much more. You will learn the proven approach that enables you to make friends, establish trust, and achieve your professional goals. It's the perfect selling system for today's marketplace.

Published by Simon and Schuster, 126 pages, paperback

■ Brilliant Thoughts &
Provocative Questions

This book is a treasury of universal truths
and life-transforming insights from some
of the world's greatest thinkers and leaders
— sprinkled with intriguing questions that
invite you to reflect more deeply upon
the wisdom contained within the quotes.
The book is arranged according to topic,
allowing more focused contemplation of the
ideas. Included are chapters on compassion,
purpose, gratitude, magnificent kindness,
living creatively, manifesting your power, and
other profound themes.

*Published by Joy of Living Publishing, 122 pages,
hardcover*

CPSIA information can be obtained
at www.ICGtesting.com
Printed in the USA
FFHW020711110819
54188534-59906FF